handguns

handguns

Frederick Wilkinson

A COLLECTOR'S GUIDE TO PISTOLS AND REVOLVERS FROM 1850 TO THE PRESENT

CHARTWELL
BOOKS, INC.

A QUINTET BOOK

Published by Chartwell Books
A Division of Book Sales, Inc.
110 Enterprise Avenue
Secaucus, New Jersey 07094

This edition produced for sale
in the U.S.A., its territories
and dependencies only.

ISBN 1-55521-916-0

This book was designed and produced by
Quintet Publishing Limited
6 Blundell Street
London N7 9BH

Creative Director: Richard Dewing
Designers: Roy White, Chris Dymond
Project Editor: Stefanie Foster
Editor: Lydia Darbyshire
Photographers: Paul Forrester,
Harry Rinker Junior, Chas Wilding

*Special thanks to Paul Cornish and
Paul Forrester*

Typeset in Great Britain by
Central Southern Typesetters, Eastbourne
Manufactured in Singapore by
Eray Scan Pte. Ltd.
Printed in Singapore by
Star Standard Industries (Pte) Ltd

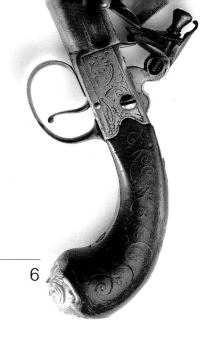

Contents

Introduction

If auctions and arms fairs are any indication, antique firearms are the most popular items among collectors of arms and armour and there seems to be a particular attraction to handguns.

The basic concept at the root of all handgun design was how to propel a piece of metal through the air on a predictable course at an appropriate speed for its intended purpose – in other words, how to fire a shot. Having achieved this goal, the next step was to devise methods of repeating the process quickly, reliably and simply. There were numerous other considerations involved in how to do the job in the most efficient way and the flood of handguns designed and produced over the last 125 years is proof of the effort devoted to these tasks.

Until the middle years of the 19th century each gun was basically unique – the product of a group of craftsmen who were masters of their trade. During the same period, however, mass-production techniques were beginning to replace the craftsman. Samuel Colt started the process in the gun trade,

and, once started, it gathered momentum until almost the only handmade firearms produced today are superb British sporting guns and rifles and the products of a few custom gunmakers.

Mass production did not, however, mean that skill and craftsmanship were completely swept away, for the engraving and decoration of guns was still carried out by gifted and skilled engravers and inlayers, nor did it mean the loss of individuality, for the history of firearms is dotted with individuals who, by one invention or patent, changed the concept of discharging a missile. There has been a host of designers, inventors and, it must be said, cranks, who thought that they could produce a gun that was better than all others or thought they could see a market that had not been exploited.

By the 1860s only one step was needed to usher in the modern handgun, and that was to replace the smoky, somewhat unreliable propellant, gunpowder. This final step was the discovery in 1886 of smokeless powder, and with this discovery came

Above

A fine example of a mid-18th-century flintlock pistol. The butt, which is decorated with inlaid silver wire, has a silver butt cap. The barrel is shaped rather like a cannon barrel and it had to be unscrewed so that the powder and ball could be loaded. In good condition such a piece is likely to be fairly expensive – probably around £600–800/$900–1,200.

the modern cartridge and the development of better and more powerful propellants.

The skill, ingenuity and time devoted to the making of a handgun attracts many collectors, and there are many possible approaches to the hobby. It is possible to specialize in a type – military revolvers or military self-loading weapons, or the weapons of a country or period, or particular calibres are just some of the more obvious ones. Many of these categories can be subdivided into such groups as target weapons, pocket pistols, police weapons, those produced by a particular company, pinfire, rimfire, percussion, single action, double action and the various operating systems of self-loading pistols. Some collectors cast a wide net and simply look for any type that pleases them.

Finally, if they are honest, many collectors have within them a streak of romanticism, which associates the handgun with a particular event, period or military action. There is also the aesthetic pleasure that comes from handling a well-balanced, smoothly functioning handgun, and for those without romance there is always the mechanics of the weapon system. Despite the frequent accusation, very few collectors are frustrated action men!

Below

A Colt Officer Model .38in revolver, of the kind that was produced between c.1908 and 1930. The date may be deduced from the stamp on the side of the barrel, which varied somewhat during the production cycle. The revolver was manufactured in a variety of calibres and with barrels of different lengths. The .32in calibre models are comparatively rare, but the .38in calibre versions are common.

Right

Many countries designated different styles of weapon by the word "Model"; in Britain the word "Mark" is used, with minor changes in design indicated by the use of a star (*). This Webley .455in Revolver Mark I was officially approved for use by the British Army on 31 January 1890. It had a 4in (10cm) barrel, and the six-shot cylinder had a self-ejecting system for empty cases. It fired a heavy bullet, a .455in calibre, and saw service in many of Britain's colonial wars. The ring at the base of the butt was for attaching a lanyard. Large numbers of the weapon were produced, and good examples may still be found.

Left

A reminder of a vanished country – an East German Makarov 9mm Pistole M. It was based on a Russian design, and Makarov-type pistols were issued to many of the police and armed forces of East European countries. Since the dissolution of the Warsaw Pact, large numbers of these and similar weapons have appeared in the West.

Hand-to-hand combat makes heavy demands on the numbers of men involved in battle. To have any chance of victory, one side needs to have better trained fighters, a larger army, or better planning and a superior strategy. There is one way, however, in which the effectiveness of each soldier can be increased and that is through the use of missile weapons. One warrior can then utilize several weapons, such as spears or arrows, one after the other, thus effectively increasing the size of the army. Such missiles also give the warrior a chance to engage the enemy at a distance.

as the devil's powder, black powder and, finally, gunpowder, was to change warfare.

At first its special qualities were not fully appreciated and gunpowder was used simply to generate a bright flash, a cloud of smoke and some noise. It was soon realized, however, that there was potential for using its power to propel a missile. Hollow bamboo tubes, reinforced with leather binding, served as barrels. One end was blocked and a small hole drilled through the side near the closed end. A quantity of gunpowder was poured down the tube, and a ball of clay – later it was to be of iron or lead – was placed on top of the powder and rammed down by a rod. When a flame was applied to the en-

The problem with such a highly effective weapon as the bow is that the archer must be strong and trained before he can become a really effective unit. Although the cross bow required less training, it was slower in use and more difficult to make. What was required was a missile weapon that was both simple to construct and easy to use and the origins of such a weapon were found in distant China.

Some time during the 11th century a group of dissimilar substances – charcoal (burnt wood), sulphur (an evil-smelling yellow substance) and saltpetre (potassium nitrate) – were combined in a unlikely mixture. This peculiar compound, which was to be known

Above

A boxlock pocket flintlock pistol made by T. Ketland and dating from the late 18th century. The butt is decorated with inlaid silver wire, and the trigger guard slides forwards to lock the action so that it may be carried safely.

closed powder through the small opening at the side – the touchhole – the powder inside burnt rapidly, generating large volumes of gas, which expanded and ejected the projectile with some force.

Barrels of iron and brass were soon developed, and the gun was born. Details of the discovery spread slowly across the known world and appear to have reached Europe in the late 13th or early 14th century. An English manuscript of 1326 shows a knight igniting the powder in a crude cannon. In the early days gunpowder was used

almost exclusively in cannon and mainly for breaching castle walls. Such guns were large and basically static, although they were soon mounted on wheeled carriages to give them mobility.

Later in the 14th century the word handgun seems to have been used for the first time. The early examples were apparently little more than small versions of cannon barrels fitted to the ends of wooden shafts or tillers. These weapons were fired manually by applying the glowing tip of a piece of cord – the match – to the touchhole. The system was improved early in the 15th century when the match was applied by a simple moving arm fitted to the side of the tiller. This curved arm, which was known as the serpentine, was later propelled forwards by pressure on a small lever or trigger. To ensure fairly certain ignition, the touchhole was mounted above a small pan fitted on the side of the barrel into which was placed a pinch of fine-grained gunpowder – the priming. It was into this that the glowing tip of the match was pressed and the ensuing flash passed through the touchhole to initiate ignition.

These handguns must have been fairly inaccurate because it was almost impossible

to aim the projectile, but changes in the shape of the stock soon allowed the butt of the weapon to be placed against the shoulder so that the firer could look along the barrel and aim the bullet. By the 16th century a practical musket had been developed. The barrel was generally about 4 feet (1.2m) long, tubular and smooth on the inside, and it fired a lead ball approximately ¾in (2cm) in diameter. Although the musket was unpredictable, it had the great virtue of simplicity. It was both fairly easy and quick to train a man in its use, and even in the hands of poorly trained soldiers a volley from a number of these weapons pointed at the enemy was certain to produce some casualties.

Above

A brass-barrelled flintlock holster pistol from around 1800 or later. The lock is marked "London Warranted", which suggests that it is a trade gun made for sale or barter with the British colonies or other countries. The standard of workmanship is competent, but little more, and such pieces are not greatly valued and may be acquired from specialist dealers at reasonable prices. Similar items were still being made in Belgium until the late 19th century.

This matchlock musket was heavy and cumbersome, and its use was somewhat limited in that to be ready for instant action the match had to be glowing at all times. It was also potentially dangerous, since its use meant that there were numerous glowing matches within the vicinities of gunpowder, and any stray spark could have disastrous results. The need to have a match burning for long periods meant that it was very difficult to carry the weapon ready for action without constantly replacing the match as it burnt away. There was certainly no way in which a matchlock weapon, primed and ready for use, could be carried in a pocket or holster.

By sometime late in the 15th century and certainly by the early 16th century an improved system of ignition had been developed. Gone was the glowing match, in its place was a mechanical device that generated a shower of sparks to ignite the powder. This device was known as the wheel-lock, since the sparks were generated by the friction of the roughened edge of a rotating wheel pressing against a piece of mineral known as pyrites. The energy to rotate the wheel was provided by a strong spring which had to be spanned or put under tension by turning a key or spanner. The mechanism was mounted in the wooden stock, and with its appearance the true handgun or pistol became possible, as small firearms, loaded and ready to fire, could now be safely carried in a pocket, bag or holster. It was soon appreciated that these new weapons constituted a serious security problem, since an assassin could conceal a weapon until he was close to his unsuspecting target. As early as 1517 Emperor Maximilian I of Austria (1459–1519) enacted restrictive laws against the carrying of self-igniting handguns — an early example of legal restrictions on firearms, a process that continues today.

Below

A top quality flintlock pistol by the London maker William Parker. It was produced about 1820. Such items may be readily acquired from dealers and auction houses, although not all examples will be in such fine condition as the one illustrated.

Left

This double-barrelled, tap action, boxlock, flintlock pistol dates from c.1800. It is described as boxlock because the cock holding the flint is centrally mounted instead of being at the side as is more usual. Tap action refers to the selection of the barrel to be fired, which is done by means of the ring mounted on the side. The pistol illustrated was made in Belgium, but similar examples were produced in Britain, and they are not expensive.

The origin of the name pistol is a matter of debate. Some historians say it derives from the town of Pistoia in Tuscany, Italy, while others hold that it comes from the name of a small pipe-like whistle. Whatever its origin, the word soon came to mean a small, portable firearm that could be used in one hand.

The main problem with the wheel-lock was its complexity. The mechanism was fairly intricate and liable to jam and break down, and when this happened the services of a fairly skilled craftsman were required to effect repairs. The complexity also made it expensive to manufacture, and the high cost prevented its general issue to all troops, although some cavalry regiments and body-guards were armed with wheel-lock pistols. Gunmakers were always looking for a mechanism that could generate the vital sparks in a simpler, cheaper way. The answer was to be the flintlock.

Friction was still used to produce the sparks, but instead of the wheel and pyrites, the mechanism used a wedge-shaped piece of flint, which was scraped against a flat steel plate. The principle was not new – it had been used in various forms on firearms during the 16th century – but it was not until the 17th century that the mechanism known as the flintlock really came into its own.

The commonest form, known as the French-lock, used an L-shaped steel plate – the frizzen – pivoted at the tip of the shorter arm. This was mounted just above the pan, and when it was closed the lower, shorter section covered the pan and its priming powder. A curved arm – the cock – which had two adjustable jaws at the top to hold the flint, was impelled by a V spring and swung forwards to scrape the thin end of the flint down the longer arm. This caused it to tilt forwards to uncover the priming just as the friction of flint and steel generated the sparks, which fell into the priming and fired the gun. The internal mechanism was simpler than that of the wheel-lock and con-sequently sturdier and a great deal cheaper to produce. With minor improvements and modifications, the flintlock remained the

Above

The pistol was loaded by unscrewing the barrel and pouring the powder directly into the breech. The ball was placed on top and the barrel was screwed back into position. This system did away with the ramrod, and it was often used on flintlock and percussion pocket pistols.

main firearm ignition system for the next two centuries. Reliable and durable, it functioned well whether it was mounted on a musket, a large wall-gun or a pistol small enough to drop into a pocket. Modifications to improve its reliability and speed of function were made, and it was fitted with various devices to prevent accidental discharge. It was versatile and was adapted for a wide range of uses on various weapons.

Despite its many advantages, the flint-lock still suffered from some serious drawbacks, not least its vulnerability to wind and weather. Rain could dampen the priming and the wind could blow it away, both circumstances rendering the weapon useless. There was another less obvious but nonetheless frustrating feature. Each of the individual actions involved in igniting the powder and firing a shot took up a small amount of time, but when they were added together these small periods represented an appreciable delay between the pressing of the trigger and the firing of the shot. In battle, with massed volleys of fire, this time lag – the hangfire – was of little importance, but for the sportsman, who was firing at a moving target, it was un unwelcome complication for which he had to make an allowance when aiming. Various attempts to overcome the problem were made, but it fell to a Scottish cleric, Alexander Forsyth, to produce the practical answer – the percussion system.

Forsyth dispensed with the pan and priming powder and substituted a solid-nosed hammer for the flint cock. By means of an ingenious device he deposited a few grains of unstable chemicals, known as fulminates, at the mouth of a short tube leading to the touchhole. Pressing the trigger allowed the hammer to fall forwards and strike the grains of fulminate, which exploded, and the resulting flash passed along the tube through the touchhole and ignited the charge. By this means the hangfire was reduced as was the number of misfires, which were often caused by worn flints.

Forsyth patented his system in 1807 and travelled to London where he opened a shop to sell his new percussion guns. The idea was good, but his method of depositing the fulminate above the touchhole was a trifle too complex and just a little dangerous. Many inventors produced alternative systems, but it was not until the 1820s that a really practical solution was developed – the percussion cap. This was a small copper thimble with a layer of fulminate crystals deposited on the inside at the top. The cap was placed over a tubular pillar – the nipple – which led to the touchhole, and when it was struck by the hammer the fulminate flashed to ignite the charge. It was simple and effective, and it was to change the design of firearms and lead eventually to the modern handgun.

2

Revolvers

Below

This early percussion revolver is one of a type usually described as transitional, because they come between the pepperbox and the true percussion revolver. This example, possibly made by the British maker Brazier, has a coarse-threaded securing fitting to the cylinder. This was designed to permit the swift removal of an empty cylinder and its replacement with a loaded one. Examples of this kind of revolver are not uncommon, and they may be acquired for reasonable outlay.

The invention of the percussion cap opened up new horizons for gunmakers, but the biggest changes probably occurred in the design of multi-shot weapons. The flintlock had been just a little too awkward to adapt to weapons firing more than three or four shots. Some flintlock revolvers had been made, but they were expensive to produce, rather cumbersome and not too reliable.

The man responsible for the biggest advances was an American from Connecticut whose name has become almost synonymous with the revolver – Samuel Colt (1814–62). Although he did not invent the revolver, for it had been known since the 16th century, Colt revolutionized the design and, even

more importantly, introduced a system of mass production for such weapons. He produced a revolver with a cylinder that was drilled with five or six chambers, each with its own short tube or nipple to hold a percussion cap. Pulling back the hammer activated a simple linkage system, which rotated the cylinder and brought a loaded chamber into line with the barrel. Pressing the trigger allowed the hammer to fall forwards and strike the uppermost cap and so fire the first shot. The process could be repeated until all the shots were discharged.

Colt's first venture into the arms business was not a great success, but by luck and

Right

Pulling back the hammer rotates the cylinder so that the next unfired charge lines up with the barrel.

Above

*A Dragoon 3rd Model
Percussion Revolver with
Holster c1853/4. This
weapon belonged to
Captain Francis T. Bryan
of the U.S. Army and saw
service on the American
frontier. A heavy weapon,
it fired a bullet of .44in
calibre. The cylinder was
engraved with a scene of a
fight with American
Indians. All of Colt's early
revolvers were single
action, which means that
the hammer had to be
pulled back before the
trigger could be pressed to
fire the weapon.*

perseverance he remained in business, and in 1848 he produced the heavy Dragoon revolver, which fired six shots of .44in calibre. He continued to manufacture this weapon with minor constructional differences over the next few years, ceasing production in 1861. In 1848 he also began supplying a smaller version, the Pocket Colt, which fired a .31in diameter bullet. The design was slightly modified in 1849, and this model remained in production until about 1873.

In 1851 he introduced the larger Belt pistol, which is more commonly known as the Navy Colt, with a calibre of .36in, and this was also kept in production until about 1873. It was an accurate and reliable pistol, and about 40,000 were produced.

In 1851 the Great Exhibition of Trade and Industry was held in London's Hyde Park, and Colt decided to attend and display his products. By dint of presenting examples of his revolver to well-known public figures and through publicity and general showmanship he made a great impact on the British market, to the annoyance of the British gunmakers. They were even more upset when he set up

a factory in Pimlico, London, to manufacture his revolvers.

All of these early Colt revolvers conform to a general style, with a cylinder engraved with an appropriate scene – a hold-up on the Pocket, a naval battle on the Navy Colt and a fight with Indians on the Dragoon revolver, for example. The barrels, which were produced in a variety of lengths, were stamped with varying legends, including an address. These markings make it possible to distinguish those produced in the London factory from the American-produced weapons, although some interchanging of parts did take place.

In 1856 Colt started production of his New Model Pocket revolver, which featured a side-mounted hammer for easy maintenance, but in 1861 he reverted to the old style with a Pocket Model but of the Navy calibre, .36in. In 1860 he made a larger, .44in calibre revolver, known as the New Model Army or Holster pistol, and this featured a round barrel with a loading lever that was used to press down the bullet into the chamber, which was streamlined into the barrel housing. He used a similar styling for his new Navy revolver in .36in calibre as well as on the Police Model.

Colt's London factory did not survive long but, stimulated by his example, many British manufacturers began to explore the revolver market. One of the leading makers was Robert Adams, who was soon in production with a large calibre percussion revolver. The design of the Adams revolver differed from those made by Colt in many respects, but one major difference was in the method of firing. Colt's revolvers were all single action, which means that to fire a shot the hammer had to be pulled back manually, usually with the thumb. At the first click – the half cock – the cylinder could be rotated freely for loading, and, when ready, the hammer was pulled further back and locked in this position, which is known as cocked. The trigger was then pressed and the hammer, driven by a spring housed in

Right and Below

A French Pistolet de Marine made about 1840. It has a back-action percussion lock, a lanyard ring on the butt and a swivel ramrod for loading. The pistol has a belt hook on one side, and this could be pushed through the sailor's belt to leave his hands free. The lock plate is inscribed "Manufre Rol de Chatellerault", the arsenal at which it was produced. These rather plain percussion pistols are not keenly collected and they are available at reasonable prices.

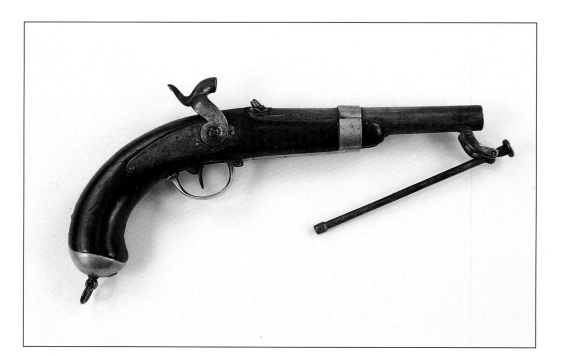

Colt

Some Colt revolvers were specially engraved, and these are obviously very desirable to collectors and realize quite high prices. The main components of Colt revolvers were stamped with a number, and those weapons of which all the parts bear the same number are more highly prized than those with mixed numbering. A great deal of research on the history of Colt revolvers has been undertaken, and there are several reliable books, which can help to date and identify the many variations and styles of these very popular handguns.

Above

A Colt Single Action Army Revolver, which has been in production for longer than almost any other handgun. Introduced in 1873, it is still made today. This example is unusual in that the calibre is .357in Magnum, and only a comparatively small number of this type was manufactured.

the butt, swung forwards to fire the shot. Adams's early revolvers had no spur on the hammer, which could be cocked manually only with great difficulty. Pressure on the trigger rotated the cylinder, cocked the hammer and, as pressure was maintained, allowed it to fall forwards, to fire the weapon.

There was much debate as to which was the better system, and cogent arguments were provided on both sides. It was claimed that single action made for more careful shooting, while Adams's system enabled more rapid fire but required greater pressure on the trigger, which made aiming more difficult because the revolver tended to turn slightly in the hand. Adams soon went one better. Using a mechanical system patented by Lieutenant Frederick Beaumont, he produced a double action weapon, which could be fired using either method, but Colt continued to use his single action design.

Another great British gunmaker was William Tranter, and he attempted, with one model, to combine the virtues of both actions in one system with his double trigger revolver. The trigger was longer than usual, and the end protruded through the guard. Pressure on this lower section rotated the cylinder

Above

Produced from 1871 until 1876, the Colt House pistol preceded the Single Action Army Revolver in the development of metallic cartridge revolvers. Because of the shape of the cylinder, the four-shot version was known as the Cloverleaf model. Several versions were made in .41in long or short rimfire, and some were issued with ordinary round cylinders. Fewer than 10,000 were produced, and there is some interest among collectors in this particular model.

Gun Cases

Most revolvers could be purchased as separate items, but many were sold in wooden cases, the inside of which was divided into a series of compartments, each holding one item essential for using the weapon. The majority of cases held a powder flask, a bullet mould for casting the lead bullets and a key for unscrewing the nipples; most included a cleaning rod, and some held spare cylinders, oil bottles and tins for caps and bullets. The inside of the lid normally carried the maker's printed trade label and often instructions on the care and use of the revolver.

Above

A percussion revolver produced by William Tranter, a well-known British gunmaker. This 120-bore example has a double-trigger action. The longer section rotates the cylinder and cocks the action, while the portion inside the trigger guard actually fires the shot. The side-mounted ramrod was used during loading to force the bullet down into the chamber. In good condition a similar example would cost about £300/$450.

and cocked the action. Once cocked the revolver could be held at the aim and light pressure on the upper part enclosed within the trigger guard fired the shot.

Other British makers produced percussion revolvers, and their names will be found stamped on the barrels or frames. Many enjoyed a comparatively short spell as manufacturers, but others achieved worldwide renown. The names Lang, Deane, the London Armoury Company, Baker, Daw,

Harding and W. Parker will all be found on a number of percussion revolvers, and that of Webley survived until well into this century.

British gunmakers were not the only manufacturers stirred by Colt's success, and in the United States there was an upsurge of revolver production, which was further stimulated by the Civil War (1861–5). A variety of styles and patents was used, some of which blatantly copied the look of Colt's products while others broke fresh ground.

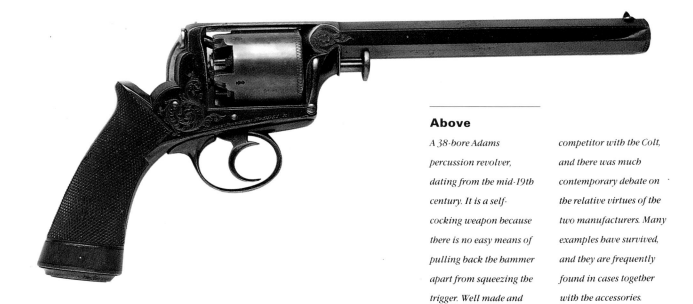

Above

A 38-bore Adams percussion revolver, dating from the mid-19th century. It is a self-cocking weapon because there is no easy means of pulling back the hammer apart from squeezing the trigger. Well made and sturdy, this was a direct

competitor with the Colt, and there was much contemporary debate on the relative virtues of the two manufacturers. Many examples have survived, and they are frequently found in cases together with the accessories.

Left

A Nagant 7.62mm revolver. First made in 1892, it was adopted by the Russian Army in 1895 and remained in service throughout World War II. It uses a special cartridge, which has the bullet sealed inside the metal case. When the action is cocked, the cylinder is pushed forwards a little so that the end of the barrel is seated slightly inside the chamber, which ensures an almost completely gas-tight seal. The revolver was available in both single action and double action versions.

Above

Although it bears a superficial resemblance to a Colt, this pocket percussion revolver bears the mark "London Pistol Company" on the barrel. It was made in the United States by the Manhattan Pistol Company, and the company's reasons for choosing this name for its revolvers are something of a mystery.

Firms such as Allen and Wheelock were in business only between 1857 and 1864 but supplied over 20 different model revolvers. The Bacon Manufacturing Company of Norwich, Connecticut, lasted from 1858 until 1867, producing percussion revolvers not dissimilar to Colt's Police Model.

Another Colt look-alike was produced by J. H. Cooper of Pittsburgh, Pennsylvania, but there was one very big difference for it had a double action mechanism, a feature revealed by the trigger, which requires a long pull and so sits further forwards inside the guard than the normal Colt style. Despite its name, the London Pistol Company was an American manufacturer, and the weapons were also made by the Manhattan Firearms Manufacturing Company.

An adventurous manufacturer was John Walch of New York City who patented a system of 10- and 12-shot revolvers, but his output was small. In 1859 Alexandre Le Mat of New Orleans produced a percussion revolver, which had a shot barrel mounted below the normal pistol barrel. It was not a new idea and had been used by other makers some years before. The output of his weapons in America was limited, most of his revolvers

A Cooper Double Action percussion revolver of .31in calibre, bears a close resemblance to a Colt Pocket revolver, but the position of the trigger indicates that it is a double action weapon. Pulling the trigger rotates the cylinder, cocks the action and then fires the shot. This example, Number 6526, post dates 1864 when the company moved to Philadelphia. Good examples are sought after by collectors.

Above

This revolver by Casimir Lefaucheux is a pinfire weapon, as may be seen by the slits in the rear of the cylinder. Many pinfire revolvers were manufactured in Europe, and this type and similar examples are fairly common. Pinfire weapons excite surprisingly little interest among collectors, and they are frequently available at reasonable prices.

being made in Europe. Many of the other names that first appeared around the mid-19th century were to fade rapidly, but others have survived and are still major producers today. Remington of Ilion, New York, was second only to Colt in the manufacture of revolvers and made over 14 different models. It is still producing firearms today.

During the American Civil War the Confederate forces were very poorly supplied with manufacturing resources, but they did succeed in producing some revolvers. The Dance Brothers of Columbia, Texas, were probably the most prolific, but there were numerous other suppliers. There is a romantic air about the Southern forces, and weapons with Confederate markings are eagerly sought after – so much so that some unscrupulous dealers and collectors have obliged by marking them with CSA and similar markings. It is as well to be very cautious when offered Confederate weapons.

Pinfire Weapons All percussion revolvers suffered from the same limitation – that is, of muzzle loading. Each chamber had to be filled with powder, a bullet rammed down on top of the powder and a cap placed on the nipple. Paper cartridges, which held one charge of powder, and a lead bullet were commonly used, but they still had to be torn open. There had been experiments with self-contained cartridges, and some had been very successful, although they had not been taken up for various reasons. However, the first really practical commercial steps were taken soon after the percussion principle had been adopted, and this was the system known as pinfire.

In 1835 the Frenchman Casimir Lefaucheux patented a system that used a metal or card cartridge case with a small hole in the side through which a short metal pin passed. The tip of the rod rested on some fulminate embedded in the powder charge contained within the case. If this pin were struck, it pressed down to detonate the fulminate and so produce an explosive flash to ignite the charge. Lefaucheux designed guns with a small slot at the breech so that when the cartridge was inserted the pin could project through it, ready to be struck by the hammer.

The pinfire system was exhibited at the Great Exhibition in London in 1851, which Colt attended, but it seems to have attracted little attention despite the fact it now made breech-loading comparatively simple. Possibly because of the impetus given by Colt's display, in 1854 Lefaucheux's son, Eugene, patented in France and Britain a revolver using the pinfire cartridge. Soon his firm was taking orders for military revolvers from several countries, including Egypt, as well as

many civilian orders. Britain and the USA showed only limited interest, but on the continent of Europe pinfire revolvers were produced in quantity and adopted by many countries for their armies. Some certainly saw service during the American Civil War. Large numbers were manufactured for the civilian market and were often sold in cases with a range of accessories. Many revolvers were produced that had, as a safety measure, triggers that folded back to reduce the chances of snagging on clothing or a container.

The ease of loading a metal pinfire cartridge encouraged many European makers to design revolvers with large cylinders hold-

Above

Typical of the cheaper form of firearm available in the latter part of the 19th century is this pinfire pepperbox revolver, which was made in Liège, Belgium. It consists of a cylinder, a simple butt and a folding trigger, which operates a flat hammer. Such weapons, primarily intended for self-defence, are usually of small calibre, but this is of 7mm calibre.

Above

The long barrel on this .22in Smith & Wesson single shot pistol indicates that it is primarily a target weapon. It is a top break

pistol and the first examples of this weapon were made on modified revolver frames but later the frame was altered. There were four main

types produced although all are similar. On the whole, single shot weapons do not seem to appeal to most collectors.

ing as many as 12 or 20 shots. A few had even more, although some became so bulky as to defeat their own purpose. Some makers, such as the French manufacturer Jarre, replaced the cylinder with a flat bar drilled with chambers. Because of its shape, this is usually known as a harmonica gun.

Small revolvers composed of little more than the cylinder and a nominal barrel were fitted inside purses and small boxes, and one was combined with a folding knife and knuckle duster to make the so-called Apache pistol. Other small versions were mounted in walking sticks to offer a disguised self-defence weapon.

The majority of pinfire handguns were made in Belgium at the manufacturing town of Liège, and they may be easily recognized by the proof mark with the letters ELG, which are stamped into the frame and/or the cylinder.

Rimfire Cartridges The pinfire represented a significant step forwards, but it had its limitations. The slot in the breech or chamber was a slight handicap, and the projecting pin represented a potential danger because an accidental knock could produce an unwanted shot. The system had, however, demonstrated the potential for the use of cartridges containing their own means of ignition. It was the far-sighted partnership of two famous names that made the next and crucial step. Horace Smith and Daniel Wesson, who were both from Massachusetts, were involved in the production of firearms, and in 1852 they joined forces and explored the possibilities of the Hunt bullet, which had been patented in 1848. This was basically a lead bullet with a hollow base that was filled with propellant and covered by a disc with a central hole to allow ignition. The partners developed the idea and incorporated

the concept of the Flobert cartridge, which was really only a percussion cap with a small lead ball pressed into the open end.

By 1856 Smith & Wesson had perfected the general design for a revolver that would take a metal cartridge loaded from the rear of the cylinder. They came to an agreement with an ex-employee of Colt, Rollin White, who had patented a revolver in which the chambers in the cylinder were drilled right through. This meant that the cartridge could be loaded from the rear. The cartridge had a small hollow rim, which held a deposit of fulminate, and when it was placed in the chamber the rim rested against the end of the cylinder. When the hammer fell it compressed the rim of the case against the end of the cylinder and detonated the fulminate to fire the charge. The modern revolver had arrived.

By 1858 Smith & Wesson were offering a .22in calibre breech-loading revolver for sale, and as they held the master patent no other gunmaker could copy the system without permission. The revolver was small, with the barrel hinged at the top and held closed by spring catches at the bottom of the cylinder housing. The cylinder was removable, and the empty cases could be pushed out using a rod fixed below the barrel. The

Above

A four-barrelled Sharps pistol, which was intended to be a weapon for self-defence. The design is ingenious – as the hammer is pulled back for each shot, the firing pin assembly rotates to

bring it in line with an unfired barrel. The fired cases were loaded and ejected by pulling the barrel block forwards. While these pistols are not common, they are not normally very expensive.

Above

It may look like a Colt Single Action Army revolver but it is a .22in version made by Ruger. This firm has become a very important

manufacturer of weapons of excellent quality. This one has a floating firing pin which is mounted in the frame and not fitted to the hammer.

weapon was well received but was some-what limited in its appeal because of its small calibre – only .22in. In addition, the cases tended to swell when fired and sometimes jammed the action.

Increasing the calibre meant using a bigger case, but the metal could not be made too thick or the hammer could not crush it to detonate the charge. By 1861 Smith & Wesson had solved the problems and were offering a .32in revolver and working on designs for a .44in weapon.

Centrefire The appearance of the Smith & Wesson revolvers established the basis of the modern handgun, but one further step was still necessary. Although the rimfire cartridge was a great improvement on pre-vious loading sequences, it did have some limitations, especially when it was used for larger calibres. Two men were working, in-dependently, towards the next big advance – in the US Colonel Berdan and in Britain Colonel Edward Boxer. The outcome of their efforts in the 1860s was the centrefire car-tridge. Instead of the fulminate compound being deposited in a thin layer over the inside

base of the cartridge case, a percussion cap was fitted into a central hole in the base of the case. The walls and base of the case could now be of any thickness, since the only part to be hit was the cap. The design of the revolver hammer was changed so that it had a sharp point rather than the flat bar that had been used on the hammers of rimfire weapons – a useful guide in deciding whether a weapon is centrefire or pinfire. Detonation was swift and effective, and loading the car-tridge was simple thanks to Rollin White's system. Thus, by the 1860s, the style of almost every future revolver had been estab-lished, and the subsequent claims of manu-facturers to have produced new models were accurate in only a limited sense.

There was still one problem to be resolved and that was how to insert the cartridges into the chambers of the cylinder. Three basic solutions were devised. On some re-volvers, such as the Colt Single Action Army, a hinged plate was fitted to the frame just behind the butt end of the cylinder. To load the revolver, this plate or loading gate was flipped sideways to reveal the chambers awaiting the cartridges. The cylinder was

Above

This Smith & Wesson .38in revolver is fitted with a trigger shoe. This is a little device used by some target shooters to afford a firmer touch on the trigger. By the side is a speed loader used to load six rounds in one movement.

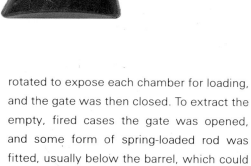

rotated to expose each chamber for loading, and the gate was then closed. To extract the empty, fired cases the gate was opened, and some form of spring-loaded rod was fitted, usually below the barrel, which could be pushed back through the chamber to eject the case. Other revolvers used a similar system, but the loading gate hinged backwards rather than sideways.

Another solution was to fit the cylinder onto a sideways swinging crane mounted in the frame. Pressing a catch released the pivoted crane so that it could be pushed sideways, taking the cylinder clear of the frame and so allowing easy access to the chambers. Extraction of the cases was effected by a star-shaped plate, located at the centre rear of the cylinder, which fitted into a shallow recess of the cylinder. A spring-loaded rod passed through the centre of the cylinder and the crane, and a push on this rod raised the star, which engaged with the rim of the case and lifted it clear of the cylinder.

The third method was to build the revolver frame in two parts, with the barrel section hinged at the base in front of the cylinder. Releasing a catch allowed the barrel to be dropped down, taking the cylinder with it

Above

Probably the best known revolver in the world, the .45in Colt Single Action Army Revolver was made in a variety of calibres and with various barrel lengths. This example has the 7½in (19cm) barrel,

which was the style adopted by the US Cavalry. Early examples command high prices, because of their association with the Old West and American Frontier life.

Below

Adopted by the French Army in 1892, a feature of this 8mm six shot revolver is that the side plate on the left swings down and forwards to allow easy access to the internal mechanism for cleaning and servicing. Large numbers of this revolver were produced and even today they are still around.

and so exposing the back ready for loading. At the same time as the barrel section was dropped, a simple linkage system pushed up the rod, which was fitted to the star-shaped end plate, so ejecting the cases. As the barrel was lowered a little further, the star piece was released and, under the pressure of a spring, snapped back into place, rendering the cylinder ready for reloading. This neat device was patented in the late 1860s by Smith & Wesson.

Because Smith & Wesson held the master patent for drilled-through cylinders, nobody could manufacture similar cylinders without their permission. There were numerous attempts to evade this restriction, and there were sundry odd law cases. However, in 1873 the master patent expired and the field was open for all the gunmakers. The Colt factory then produced its best known weapon. Listed officially as the Colt Single Action Army Revolver, it retained the traditional Colt silhouette and had a 7½in (19.5cm) barrel, although other lengths were made. It had a loading gate at the rear of the cylinder, and a spring-loaded ejector rod was housed beneath the barrel. This weapon acquired a range of titles, including the six-shooter, the Equalizer and the Frontier. It was so popular and has become so enshrined in folk memory by its appearance in films, that it has remained almost continuously in production since 1873 and has been made in a wide assortment of calibres and barrel lengths. In films and on television it has featured at the Battle of the Alamo (1836) and in the American Civil War (1861–5) – a remarkable achievement for a weapon that was not made until 1873.

The floodgates were now opened, and all the gunmakers began to produce new, breech-loading revolvers. There were in-

Below

This .32in revolver with a five-shot cylinder was available in several forms, with square or bird's head butt and with spurred hammers. The manufacturer, Mervin Hulbert & Co., was active during the 1880s, but the revolvers do not have the same romantic appeal as other weapons of the period. Most of this company's revolvers were nickel-plated.

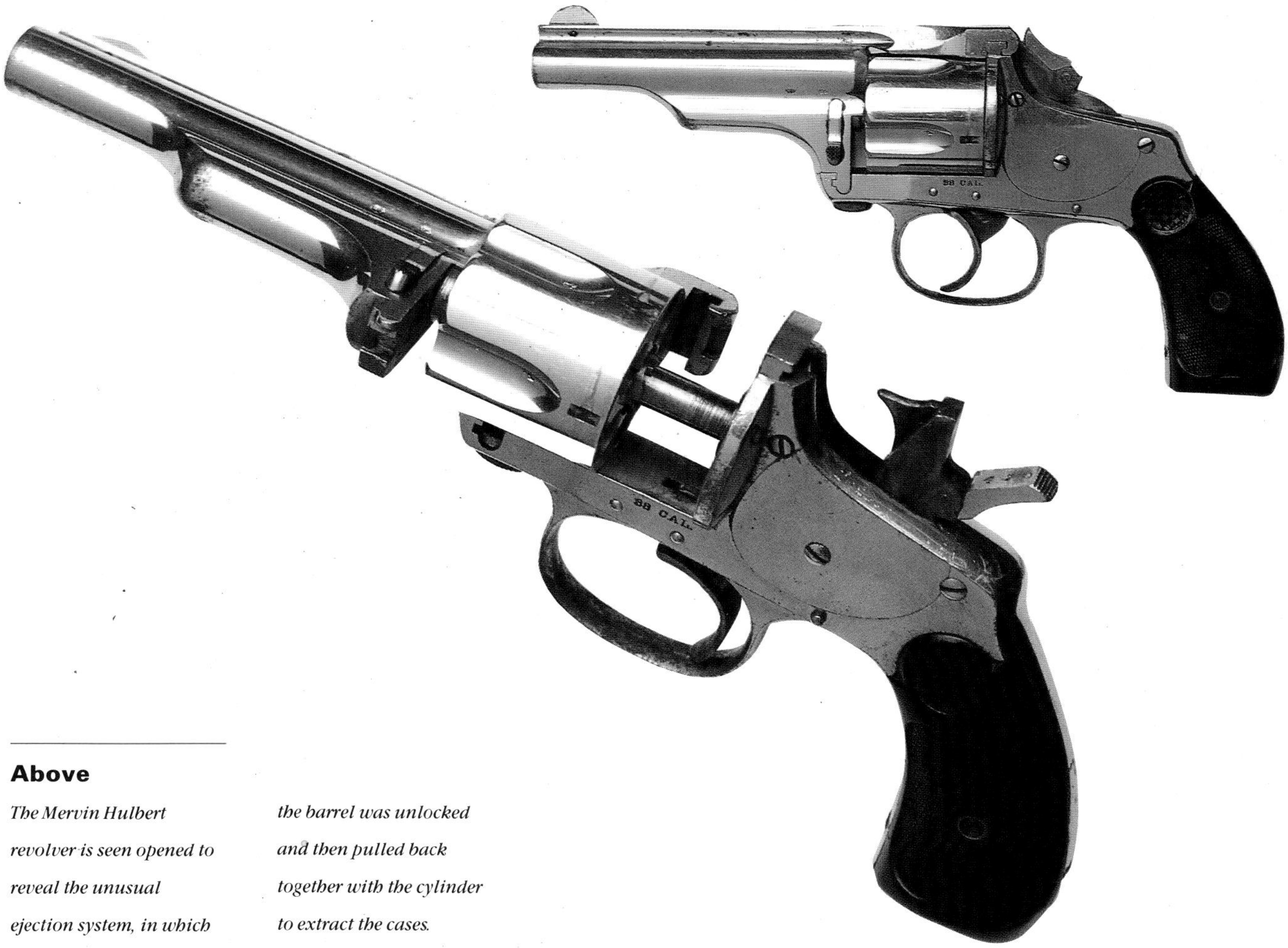

Above

The Mervin Hulbert revolver is seen opened to reveal the unusual ejection system, in which the barrel was unlocked and then pulled back together with the cylinder to extract the cases.

Above

The Spanish manufacturer Astra produced this .357in calibre revolver, which is available with various barrel lengths. The cartridge is a more powerful version of the .38in Special, which has a slightly longer case and a larger charge of powder. The longer case prevents its being loaded into the cylinder of a .38in Special revolver, which might well fracture from the greater pressure of the more powerful charge.

numerable different calibres, different barrel lengths and different grips, but all were basically similar. Some of the older rimfire, pinfire and percussion weapons were converted to the new system, and these form an interesting and very collectable group.

Many of the surviving percussion revolvers were forgotten in the excitement of acquiring the latest models, and they survive in quantity and are well collected. The early Colts are rare and are consequently the most expensive. The Paterson and Walker models are also likely to be very expensive. Although the Dragoon models are hardly common, they cannot really be described as rare, and they do turn up in auctions and with dealers. The better the condition, the more desirable the piece and the higher the price. Engraved examples of any Colt percussion revolver attract high prices, and

those with names or regimental associations are also very sought after.

British percussion revolvers appear to lack the romantic appeal of Colts and they seldom attract such high prices. There are no early rare models as with Colt, which was in production some 10–20 years before most of the British makes. However, as with Colts, condition is a vitally important factor. The colouring is important too: it must be the original colour and not one of the modern, cold blues, which, compared with the original, look dead and lacklustre.

One great virtue of all these percussion weapons is that, provided they are not going to be fired, they count as antiques and, even in countries such as Britain with its restrictive gun legislation, do not require any form of licence to keep.

Rimfire weapons are still fairly common, and the variety of models with so many minor variations manufactured by Smith & Wesson ensures that there are great possibilities for acquiring collections of a range of different weapons. However, less scrupulous manufacturers copied Smith & Wesson revolvers, and there are many look-alikes, so many, in fact, that the company had to issue leaflets warning potential buyers to check carefully. Although there are some restrictions on owning such weapons, in general there are few problems, apart from .22in calibre pistols. Serious problems arise with the cartridge weapons, and most countries have legislative

Right and Below

Remington was established in 1816 and is still making guns today. The company's production of percussion revolvers, one of which is shown here, began in 1857, and it made a variety of weapons ranging from pocket revolvers to large .44in weapons for military use.

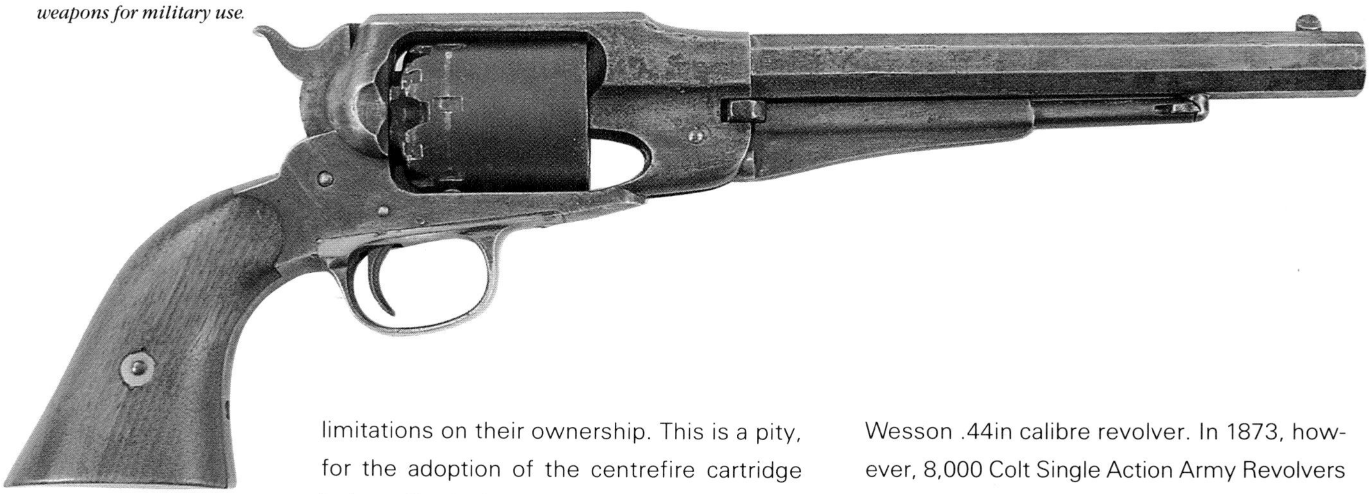

Opposite, Below

Many of the earlier handguns have been reproduced for modern shooters. The New York manufacturers Rogers & Spencer originally produced the Army Model revolver in the 1860s with a calibre of .44in. The reproduction shown here, however, is in 9mm calibre, and it uses metal cartridges instead of the original percussion caps.

limitations on their ownership. This is a pity, for the adoption of the centrefire cartridge led to a flood of models from many countries, and the number of types surviving is high.

The armed services of most countries reviewed their weapons in the light of the latest developments, and the number of military revolvers that saw service is very high. The numbers made obviously help to determine rarity, and some models are keenly sought after, but, on the other hand, many military weapons saw plenty of service and tend to be somewhat worn and rubbed, which can depress their price.

In the USA a special group, the Small Arms and Accoutrements Board, was established to evaluate the needs of the army, and in 1870 it chose, surprisingly, a single-shot Remington pistol as well as a Smith &

Wesson .44in calibre revolver. In 1873, however, 8,000 Colt Single Action Army Revolvers in .45in calibre were purchased for the US Cavalry. A year later, in 1874, 3,000 Smith & Wesson Model 3 Schofield revolvers (so-called after the officer who designed the original) were purchased, but generally the Colt seems to have been more popular with the troops.

In the 1878 model Colt deserted its long-established single action system and produced a double action revolver, but the US Army was not impressed. However, the double action system was here to stay, and many other revolver manufacturers adopted the system.

A small number of Colt percussion revolvers was ordered by the British Army in 1856, and Navy Colts stamped with the broad arrow indicating official-issue weapons are sought after by collectors today. In 1868 the British Army changed to breech-loading weapons, and many of the Adams and Colt percussion weapons were adapted to take a Boxer centrefire cartridge. As late as 1872 many units of the British Army were still being issued with single-shot percussion pistols, but after long discussions and some obstruction from the Duke of Cambridge, the Commander-in-Chief, revolvers were authorized for the Lancer units in 1877. Officers were always free to purchase their own revolvers, so that there was always a variety of weapons in service.

In August 1880 the pistol revolver B.L. Enfield (Mark 1), which fired a .45in cartridge, was officially approved for Army use. This was a break revolver – that is, when a catch at the top was released the barrel could be depressed and the star plate remained stationary in the rear position just far enough forwards for the empty case to fall clear, while any unfired cartridges, being longer, stayed in position. These revolvers were not very popular, and a number of changes were made, including the addition of a safety catch,

which is very unusual in revolver technology. These revolvers are still not uncommon, and because they are not greatly sought after they sell very reasonably at auction. Many have seen hard service, however, and may not be in very good condition.

In 1886 the famous British name of Webley made its mark on the official revolver field when a revolver produced by the company was adopted by the Royal Irish Constabulary. It was a rugged, sturdy weapon, firing a .442in cartridge, and it saw service with many police forces of the Empire, including those in Australia and South Africa. In 1887 the Webley Pistol (Mark I) was made the official revolver of the British Army. It was a .441in calibre and had a 4in (10cm) barrel with a top break. This was a reliable and sturdy weapon, and some 10,000 were ordered. This was but the first of a long line of Webley revolvers in various styles and calibres to be issued to the British Army, and some saw service during World War II.

All European nations examined their armament provision in light of the changes that had taken place, and Belgium's arms centre at Liège was kept extremely busy

Above

The British Enfield .476in B.L. revolver was designed in 1879 and tested by various units of the British Army. After a somewhat mixed reception, it was modified slightly before being adopted as the official revolver in August 1880. Service use, however, revealed more problems, and the design was further modified. The Mark II shown here was eventually adopted in 1887.

Above

The extraction system of the Enfield revolver is remarkable. When the barrel catch was released and the barrel pushed downwards, the cylinder moved forwards, but a stationary plate retained the cases so that, eventually, there was sufficient room for the empty case to fall out.

Above

This is a Belgian-made 11mm version of the Gasser revolver. These weapons were designed by the Austrian Leopold Gasser in 1869, and they saw service with the armies of the Austro-Hungarian Empire. This example is in the Montenegrin style, and such models are comparatively common since the king of Montenegro ordered all his male subjects to purchase an example. Most are crudely decorated and have grips of horn or mother-of-pearl.

Above

A close-up of the Gasser revolver, showing the simple, side-mounted ejector rod, which was used to push out the empty cases when the plate at the rear of the cylinder was pushed clear.

Above

The Webley .455/.476 W.G. Army Revolver, which was produced in slightly different forms between 1886 and c.1902. A solid weapon, intended primarily for military service, it was adapted for target shooting. The 6in (15cm) barrel was well suited for accuracy, and the high-quality action made for smooth trigger movement. These revolvers are fairly common.

Above

The Webley .455in Revolver Mark II, which was approved for service in May 1895, differed in only minor details from the Mark I. The butt has a smoother outline, and the hammer is a little more robust. There were other, less obvious modifications, and this example is shown in the "open" position, with the self-extractor ready to extract the empty cases.

Middle Below

The Webley .455in Revolver Mark III was approved for service in November 1897, and it differs from Mark I and Mark II in the chamber-release mechanism. It also has two V-shaped projections in front of the cylinder, and these were designed to ease the holstering of the revolver by stopping the cylinder snagging on the edge of the holster. Civilian versions were manufactured, and they have a flared butt instead of the usual rather pointed butt seen on the military issue.

Bottom

The changes in design of the Webley .455in Revolver Mark IV were even less obvious except in the change to the shape of the hammer. It was approved for service in October 1899. The locking slots on the side of the cylinder are wider than on earlier models. This weapon was issued in large numbers because its appearance coincided with the Boer War (1899–1902), during which it was carried by officers and non-commissioned officers.

Above

An unusual revolver, which was designed by the Frenchman Charles-François Galand, who had connections in both Belgium and England. In 1868 he patented an extraction system. When *the spur below the trigger guard was pushed down, the cylinder and barrel moved forwards. The cartridges were held back by a plate, which moved a shorter distance, allowing the cases to fall out.*

Above

A Galand revolver with the barrel and cylinder in the forward position, ready for case extraction. This model was adopted by the Russian Navy in 1870, and examples with *Russian markings may be found. They are not common, and their rather unusual extraction system makes them of special interest to collectors.*

producing revolvers for Belgium's own Army and for many others as well. One easily recognizable product was the Gasser revolver, which was made for Montenegro, a small Balkan state. Most of these are massive and have what looks like a disproportionately small butt.

Another very recognizable revolver manufactured in Liège is the Galand, which was designed by a Frenchman and adopted by the Russian Navy. The distinguishing feature is the trigger guard, which extends forwards under the barrel. Unlocked by a small catch, it swings forwards and down,

Above

Although the name Smith & Wesson immediately suggests an American weapon, this example was made by that firm primarily for Russia. The company was contracted to supply thousands of revolvers for the Russian armed forces, and Turkey later placed a contract for a thousand Second Model Russian revolvers. Surprisingly, they were intended to take the .44in Henry rimfire cartridge.

Above

The Smith & Wesson Second Model in open or break position. The trigger guard was given a spur, which was intended to offer a firmer grip for accurate shooting. These revolvers are quite keenly collected, but many are in only fair condition. This example is one of the Turkish contract weapons.

cartridges, which are longer because the bullets are *in situ*, remain in place. Returning the trigger guard to the closed position replaces the plate and makes the cylinder ready for action.

The Russians also adopted a Smith & Wesson revolver, the Model 3, Russian First Model, which was slightly modified to take the Russian .44in cartridge. A Second Model was issued later, and this has a spur extending down from the trigger guard to provide a firmer grip. Later, some of the revolvers were made in Berlin and in Tula, the centre of Russian arms manufacture.

moving the entire barrel assembly forwards. The cartridges pass through a plate at the rear of the cylinder, and this also moves forwards a short distance and then stops, but the cylinder continues to move forwards. The distance is such that empty cases are pulled clear of the cylinder but the unfired

The Webley-Fosbery

An unusual British revolver was designed by Colonel George Fosbery and made by Webley. The Webley-Fosbery was a self-cocking revolver in which the recoil drove back the upper section of the weapon, including the cylinder. As it moved back, a stud engaged with a zigzag groove cut into the face of the cylinder. This turned the cylinder and brought the next chamber in line with the barrel and at the same time cocked the action. The six shots could be fired as rapidly as the trigger could be pulled, and accuracy was helped by the fact that only a light pressure was needed to operate the trigger. It was an accurate weapon but expensive to produce, and although it saw service in South Africa during the Boer War (1899–1902), it had been more or less forgotten by World War I. It is a very popular weapon with shooters, and today is one of the most expensive of all classic revolvers.

Below

This British service revolver is an Enfield No. 2 Mk1**. The main differences between this and earlier British service revolvers are that it was a smaller calibre – .38in rather than .45in – and it was self-cocking. The hammer lacked a spur, which made it impossible to pull it back manually. The weapon, which dates from 1942, was a modified version of the Mark 1, and it was introduced in response to complaints from tank crews that the old spur hammers snagged on clothing and so on when it was carried inside vehicles. It was produced in large quantities during World War II and is common.

Above

This is a four-barrelled Lancaster Howdah pistol of .577in calibre. Its name derived from the story that it was carried by tiger hunters in India, who

travelled in the howdah on an elephant and who kept the pistol as a defence against any tiger that might leap onto the elephant's back. As the

trigger was pulled, an internal striker rotated to detonate each cartridge in turn.

Left

The Lancaster was designed as a top-break weapon for easy loading, but it was criticized because the trigger pull was said to be excessive and because the weapon was top heavy. Some versions were therefore made with an extra trigger to facilitate cocking. The romance associated with these weapons has made them popular among collectors, and they are not at all common.

In 1895 the Russians changed to a smaller calibre weapon, the Nagant gas seal revolver. This weapon, which was designed by a Frenchman, is very unusual in that the bullet is totally enclosed within the metal case and the neck is slightly tapered. When it is loaded the tip of the cartridge projects slightly beyond the end of the cylinder. If the action is cocked the entire cylinder is pushed forwards, which means that the tip of the cartridge engages with the barrel. The idea was that in normal revolvers there has to be a slight gap between the end of the cylinder and the mouth of the barrel through which there was a considerable leakage of gas when a shot was fired. The Nagant system sealed the gap and prevented the loss of pressure. There was a single action version of the Nagant, which was issued to non-commissioned officers, and a double action model for officers. The Norwegian Army also issued it to certain of its troops.

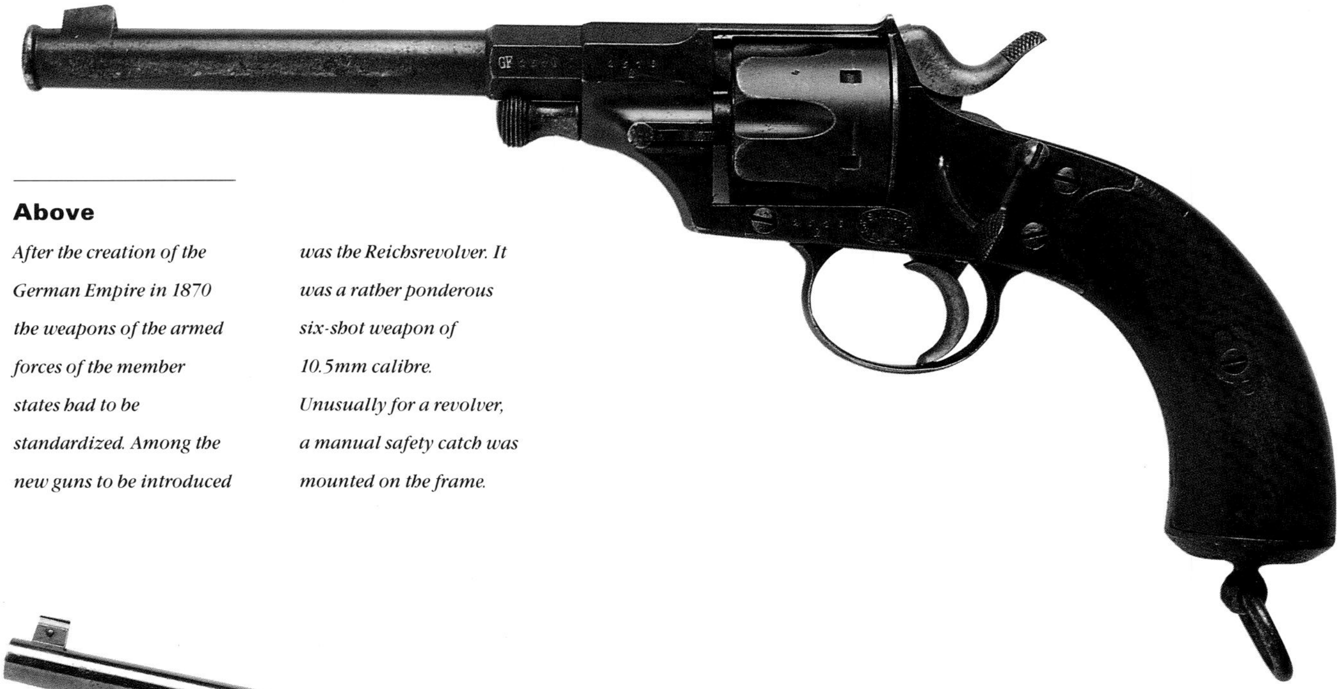

Above

After the creation of the German Empire in 1870 the weapons of the armed forces of the member states had to be standardized. Among the new guns to be introduced was the Reichsrevolver. It was a rather ponderous six-shot weapon of 10.5mm calibre. Unusually for a revolver, a manual safety catch was mounted on the frame.

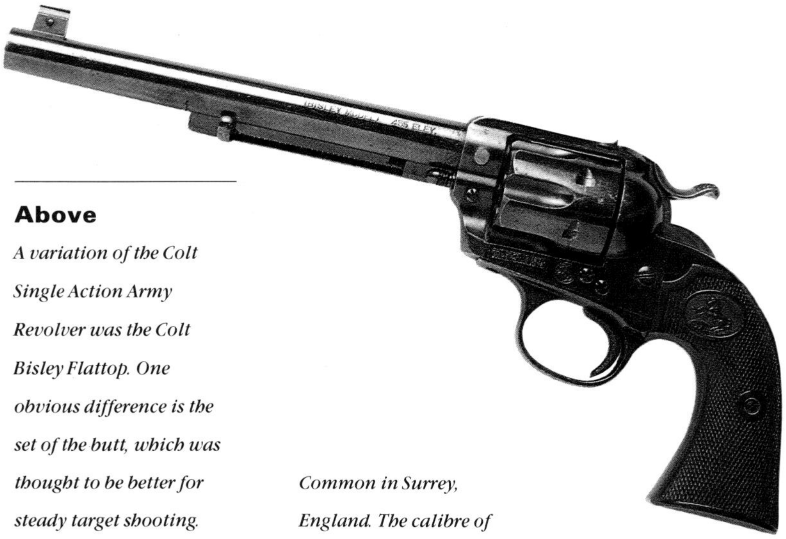

Above

A variation of the Colt Single Action Army Revolver was the Colt Bisley Flattop. One obvious difference is the set of the butt, which was thought to be better for steady target shooting. The name is derived from the ranges of the National Rifle Association on Bisley Common in Surrey, England. The calibre of this model is Eley .455in, one of the less common sizes.

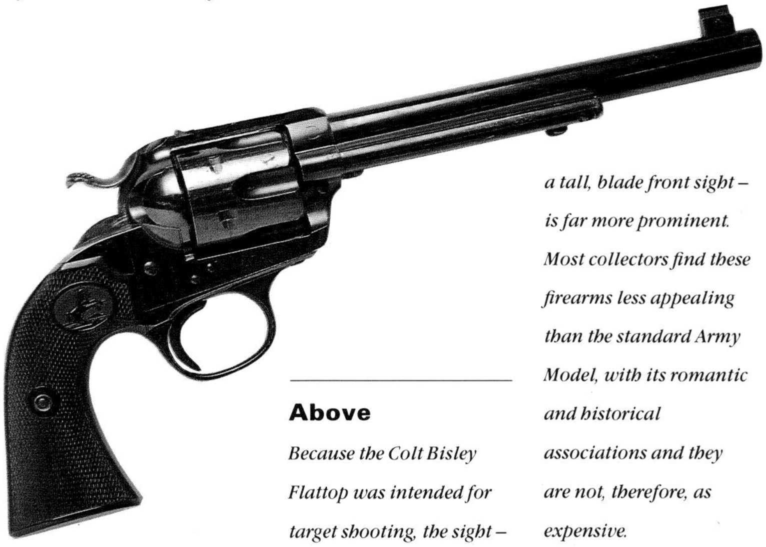

Above

Because the Colt Bisley Flattop was intended for target shooting, the sight – a tall, blade front sight – is far more prominent. Most collectors find these firearms less appealing than the standard Army Model, with its romantic and historical associations and they are not, therefore, as expensive.

One of the largest and, to many, the ugliest military revolvers is the German Reichsrevolver with its big curving butt and, for a revolver, large safety catch. It was awkward to load, but this was probably because the German Army regarded handguns as inferior weapons, to be used only in dire emergencies or by charging cavalry.

Commercial Guns In addition to all the changes in military armaments, with their emphasis on centre fire cartridge revolvers, there was also a worldwide market for commercial revolvers. Shooting as a sport was gaining in popularity, and there was a continuing growth in small bore, .22in, revolvers. Numerous companies supplied the target shooting market, particularly in the USA. Their output was considerable, and Iver Johnson of New Jersey and Harrington & Richardson Inc. of Massachusetts made thousands of small bore revolvers, most of which were top-break models with automatic ejection of the empty cases. Some manufacturers, including Smith & Wesson, Stevens and Webley, produced single-shot target guns, many of which had longer barrels to improve accuracy. They are almost invar ably single action to ensure a steady grip and easy firing, for with this action much less pressure is required to operate the trigger, and consequently the revolver is less likely to turn in the hand as the trigger is pressed. Some makers also supplied conversion sets so that a full bore revolver could be converted to fire the smaller .22in calibre. They usually include an alternative cylinder and a rifled tube, which could be inserted into the fixed barrel to reduce the bore.

Another fruitful market was for what might be called self-defence weapons. These were generally small revolvers with a calibre of .22in or .25in and small enough to drop into a pocket. There were two main types, which differed in the hammer fitting. The usual type had a spur on the hammer so that it could be cocked manually. This spur presented a potential hazard, for it could snag on clothing and possibly cock the action or even fire the revolver accidentally. The solution was the hammerless model, which had no spur to the hammer. Yet another solution was to enclose the hammer within two shielding walls, with perhaps just the tip showing so that it was possible, but not easy, to cock the action manually.

Above and Below

The Iver Johnson Safety Hammerless Revolver, which was in production between 1895 and 1950. Some people thought that the hammer of a revolver constituted a danger since it could catch on clothing and might cause the gun to be accidentally discharged. Iver Johnson produced revolvers with the hammer enclosed within the body, and these guns are referred to as "hammerless". Iver Johnson still manufactures firearms, but collectors are mainly interested in the company's early models.

Above

The 9mm Mauser Zigzag pistol is distinguished by its system of cylinder rotation. A movable stud, set in the frame, engaged with the sloping groove cut into the cylinder; as it moved fowards, it turned the cylinder. When the shot was fired, the stud returned to its original position via the straight slot.

Below

Another unusual feature of the Zigzag pistol is the upward-breaking barrel, which is released by the ring catch set near the front. The model was introduced in 1878, and its unusual design and distinctive cylinder make it popular with collectors.

Another self-defence calibre, which was more powerful and was sometimes used by police, was the .32in, and several models were produced. Although the nominal calibre was .32in, this did not mean that any revolver marked .32in would accept any .32in cartridge, for manufacturers had the habit of designing cartridges that were specific to their particular models.

Despite the proliferation of cartridges and calibres for handguns there was a gradual standardization, and today the most common calibres for revolvers can be summarized as .22in long rifle and .32in for target use and .38in Special and 9mm for general purpose such as law enforcement and some military purposes, with .44in and .45in as the largest calibres in general use. There are attempts every now and then to introduce new calibres, such as .41in and 10mm, but the others remain standard. In addition to the more or less standard ones, there are more powerful versions such as .357in Magnum, which is the .38in with a larger charge. The same applies to the .44in Magnum, which is the .44in Special with a larger charge.

From this very brief review of revolvers it must be obvious that the opportunities for "theme" acquisitions are considerable, and collections organized by calibre, type, manufacturer, nationality, military, civilian, target and action are merely some of the more obvious groups.

Above

Three versions of the Webley pistol. The example at the bottom is a .32in or 7.65mm calibre; the two examples at the top are .22in calibre. The .32in version was adopted by London's Metropolitan Police in 1911, and at the same time a .22in version was produced for them to use in practice. The cardboard ammunition boxes show both the early and modern styles.

Above

The famous Smith & Wesson Model 29 .44in Magnum revolver, which achieved fame in the film Dirty Harry *and its sequels. The revolver is made in a variety of barrel lengths, and the model illustrated is the 8⅜in (21.25cm) version, which gives the bullet a very high velocity. The recoil is heavy, and this example has been fitted with rubber grips to lessen the kick. The model is still manufactured.*

Right

A comparative newcomer to handgun production is Sturm Ruger, and the company manufactured this single action army-style revolver. The company's products have gained a reputation for good quality workmanship and reliability, and the guns incorporate many innovative approaches to manufacturing techniques. Sturm Ruger's revolvers are especially popular, and many are still in production.

By the end of the 19th century revolver design was fairly static – all the basic techniques had been mastered, and there was not much room for improvement with the materials and technology then available. Custom and convenience had settled on a basic five- or six-shot cylinder and a double action mechanism. In other fields of firearm design, however, there were great developments. One of the most important and one that was to have tremendous impact was the successful design by Sir Hiram Stevens Maxim (1840–1916) of the machine gun. The principle of self-loading firearms had been clearly demonstrated, and great interest was stimulated. If it could be done for a machine gun it could be done for a handgun: the search for such a weapon was on.

The main concept behind most self-loading weapons is that every action has an opposite and equal reaction. As the gases generated by the propellant expand and propel the bullet out of the barrel, an equal backward thrust is developed, which pushes back against the gun – the recoil. This backward thrust was one of the main methods of operating the mechanisms of many self-loading pistols. Another source of motive power was the gas generated by the propellant. If only a small amount of this gas could be diverted, it was believed, it could be used to operate a simple mechanism that would work the reloading sequence.

There is a series of actions essential to the functioning of a self-loading handgun. These actions are, in sequence:

▌ a cartridge must be picked up and loaded in the breech;
▌ the shot must be fired when required;
▌ the empty case must be withdrawn from the breech and removed from the weapon;
▌ the action must be cocked ready for the next shot so that the process can be repeated.

The first reasonably successful attempt to make a self-loading pistol occurred in 1892 at Steyr in Austria. Known as the Schonberger, it used the so-called blow-back system, but it was a rather complex version that involved using the small and critical movement of the priming cap set in the base of the cartridge. A compartment to hold six

Below

An early self-loading pistol was designed by Theodore Bergmann in 1896. This example was Bergmann's third and most successful design. The magazine, in front of the trigger guard, holds five rounds, loaded from a clip or individually. The extraction system was rather haphazard and liable to malfunction. These pistols are scarce and, therefore, expensive.

rounds of cartridges, the magazine, was located below the barrel in front of the trigger guard. Since operation depended on the small movement of the primer, the ammunition was obviously critical, and because the type available at the time was a little unreliable the action was somewhat erratic. Only a few examples were produced, and surviving examples are rare and expensive to acquire. The Bittner was a similar looking pistol but also of limited success; it was a little unusual in having a ring trigger. Another early self-loader with a similarly located magazine was the Schwarzlose, which was also patented in 1892, but another pistol by the same designer and patented in 1898 was much more "modern" in appearance.

All these early examples suffered from problems of various degrees of seriousness, but that is always the fate of early inventors in a new field. The first person to come up with a really practical, commercial self-loading pistol was Hugo Borchardt. He was born in Germany but emigrated to the United States, where he acquired a post in the Sharps Rifle Works. About 1882 he moved to Budapest, Hungary, where he also worked with firearms, but he then moved to Berlin to work for Ludwig Loewe. While there he designed a self-loading pistol in 1894.

In Borchardt's system when the shot was fired the recoil forced a metal block – the bolt – backwards for a short distance, thus operating a toggle arm. At the same time, a small hooked arm – the extractor – engaged with a groove in the base of the cartridge case, pulling it from the breech. As the bolt moved further back the case was knocked out of the extractor and clear of the gun. At the same time as the bolt was travel-

Above

Theodor Bergmann was an important figure in the early history of self-loading pistols. This example of his work is the 1908 Bergmann Bayard pistol. It was made in

Liège, and examples were supplied to Spain and Denmark. The cartridges were housed in the box magazine below the barrel, and the weapon was patented in 1903.

Below

The Schwarzlose .32in Model 1908, an Austrian-made pistol, is unusual in that the design is based on the fact that the barrel moves forwards while the slide stays in the same

position – the reverse of most self-loading systems This version has a grip safety catch fitted in front of the butt to ensure that it can be fired only when the butt is firmly gripped.

ling back it was compressing a large, curved leaf spring fitted in an oval-shaped housing at the rear of the pistol. When the bolt lost its momentum the spring took over and began to push it back towards the breech. During its forward movement the bolt pushed a fresh cartridge from the top of the magazine into the breech. At this point the bolt was locked in place and stayed so until pressure on the trigger released an internal firing pin to strike the primer and fire the shot. The bolt was then released, and the whole sequence was repeated. In a fully automatic weapon this action is repeated for as long as the trigger is pressed or until the ammunition is exhausted. Except in a very few pistols this does not happen, and a little device locks the bolt back after each shot until pressure on the trigger withdraws the locking device and the cycle can be repeated.

Lugers George Luger, who was born in Austria, was experienced in firearm design work, and he soon realized that Borchardt's system was basically sound but poorly designed, which made the weapons too bulky and heavy. He changed the spring design, removing the large oval cover section,

Above

The forerunner of the modern self-loading pistol is the Borchardt pistol, which dates from 1893 and which has a calibre of 7.63mm. This example has a non-standard type of grip on the butt; the conventional style has parallel sides. The large section at the rear houses the springs that force the breech block forwards to pick up a cartridge from the magazine and load it into the chamber. This was the model on which Luger based the design of his pistol. These pistols are rare, and, in good condition, they are likely to be very expensive.

Below

This fine example of the Artillery Luger is complete with leather holster, shoulder board and snail drum magazine. The long barrel was made to give greater muzzle velocity and improved accuracy, while the snail drum magazine ensured a high rate of fire, since it could hold 32 rounds of 9mm ammunition. This model was introduced in 1917, and it is far less common than the standard 1908 Luger. This complete set would prove expensive.

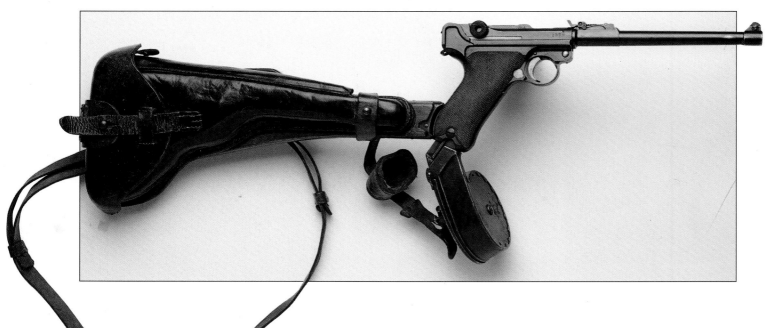

and generally lightened the weapon. By 1898 the famous Luger pistol was created. A number were manufactured by DWM, a Berlin arms company, and samples were taken by the Swiss Army for evaluation. The new pistol was found to be highly satisfactory, and in 1900 the Luger was officially adopted by the Swiss Army. The US Army purchased a thousand of the pistols, which were stamped with an American eagle, making them very rare items and highly regarded by collectors.

This new pistol had the well-known look of the Luger and a butt magazine holding eight rounds. The butt was fitted with a safety catch designed to prevent accidental discharges because the trigger would operate only if the catch were pressed, which meant, in effect, when the butt was gripped.

In the USA the pistol was tested with both a 7.65mm and a 9mm cartridge, and although its good points such as accuracy were appreciated, the weapon was rejected

because of its tendency to jam frequently. The testers also made the point that before the first shot could be fired both hands had to be used – one to grip the pistol and the other to pull back the top section – the slide – and release it in order to load the first round. This was to remain one of the drawbacks of self-loading pistols for many years until a safe system whereby the pistol could be carried with a round in the breech was devised. The negative reports led the US Army to reject the Luger, but this was not

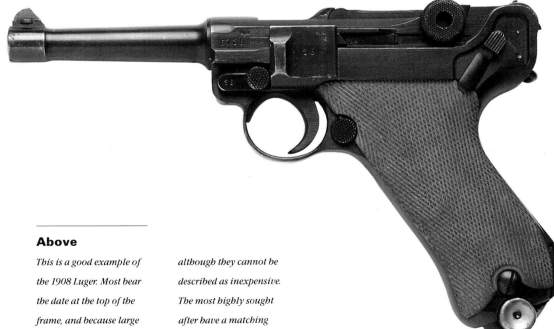

Above

This is a good example of the 1908 Luger. Most bear the date at the top of the frame, and because large numbers were produced, many have survived,

although they cannot be described as inexpensive. The most highly sought after have a matching magazine, but this is a fairly rare feature.

Above

There is a certain mystique about the Luger pistol, and many collectors and shooters are keen to own examples, even one of the more commonly found models. This specimen is a Naval Luger, which was first adopted in 1904. The models vary in detail, and apparently similar guns can fetch very different prices. There are so many tiny differences that it is essential to refer to one of the standard works on the company's products to establish rarity.

Above

Made in Czechoslovakia for the Wehrmacht during World War II, this 7.65mm Model 27 bears Nazi markings. The manufacturers, Ceska *Zbrojonka, produced large numbers between 1927 and c.1948. Those with Nazi markings are more highly sought after by some collectors.*

too much of a disappointment to the company for by then plans were well in hand to produce a commercial model using the 9mm cartridge. This model was in production by 1902, and in 1904 the German Army, like the Swiss, adopted it as its official handgun.

By 1908, after some modifications, what might be called the standard Luger self-loading pistol was in production. It had a 4in (10cm) barrel and was without the grip safety. It was produced in large quantities and in several forms. Models with longer barrels – 5½in (14cm) – were produced for the Navy, and a model for the Artillery had a 7½in (19.5cm) barrel. These two versions, like the Borchardt, were specially made so that a shoulder stock could be fitted to the butt to convert the pistol into a carbine. These models were supplied in holsters specially made to accommodate the shoulder board. There was even a fully automatic version, for which the snail drum magazine was designed to hold 32 rounds. Although it was a German weapon, it was produced at a number of arsenals, including Vickers in England.

Although Luger pistols are not uncommon, they are keenly collected for their variations. Fortunately for the collector, most are dated and carry the name of the manufacturer. The early models and unusual variants are obviously most in demand. There has been a great deal of research into the history of this weapon, and the amount of reliable, published material is considerable, enabling collectors to identify most specimens.

Mausers As is often the case, once it had been demonstrated that something is possible there is a flood of similar products, and so it was with self-loading pistols. It was obvious there was a big potential market, and many other names famous in the world of firearms began to design and produce them.

In 1896 Peter Paul Mauser designed a recoil operated pistol with a 10-round magazine, which was to become a classic firearm. So good was the mechanical system that its design was unchanged throughout its long life. Because of its rather spindly wooden grips it acquired the nickname Broomhandle.

Above

A Mauser Broomhandle pistol and stock. This version is the Schnell-Feuer, and the small plate at the side is a selector switch. When it is in one position the pistol will fire a single shot each time the trigger is pressed; when it is in the second position the pistol is fully automatic and will continue to fire as long as the trigger is pressed and there are rounds in the magazine. The wooden holster can be fitted onto the butt, and this transforms the pistol into a carbine or short rifle. This version of the Broomhandle is far less common than others, and in many countries it is regarded as a weapon that a civilian may not possess.

Left

The Broomhandle shown with the stock in position. When it was used as a carbine, it was a very accurate weapon, and when it was firing automatically it was easier to control. On full automatic fire all handguns are difficult to hold firm, and they tend to spray the shots.

Left

The butt of this Mauser Broomhandle is clearly marked with a red 9, indicating that it is chambered for 9mm cartridges. This makes it particularly attractive to collectors because, in general, this size of ammunition is more readily available than 7.63mm. All good examples of these pistols are expensive.

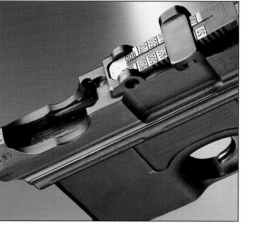

Left

A close view of the top of a Mauser 1896 pistol. The beautiful blued sight slide and the general high quality of the workmanship can be clearly seen.

Below

The 9mm Mauser Broomhandle is shown here with its wooden holster and rather complex leather carrying rig, which houses not only the pistol but also the cleaning rod. The original would be very expensive, although modern replicas of the leather rig are available.

Mauser's famous 7.63mm Broomhandle pistol has one of the best engineered locks of all pistols, the whole thing fitting together without screws, nuts or bolts. The pistol was produced with various barrel lengths, and a short-barrelled version, exported in quantity to Bolshevik Russia, became known as the Bolo Mauser. A special version with a selector catch for single shot or fully automatic fire was made, and this was known as the Schnell-Feuer. Another version was designed to accept the 9mm Parabellum cartridge made for the Luger, and this model is distinguished by having a red painted and carved figure 9 on the butt. All these pistols, including copies made by the Spanish firm Astra, were supplied in a wooden holster, which was designed to serve as a shoulder stock for the pistol.

To load this pistol the slide is pulled back and the tip of the clip inserted in the magazine, which is situated in front of the trigger. The rounds are pushed down into the magazine and the clip is discarded. The Schnell-Feuer was made with separate magazines so that an empty magazine could quickly be replaced.

Although the mechanical system remained unaltered, minor modifications were made, and the earlier models are highly prized. Mauser 96 is such a well-made pistol that it is admired and treasured by collectors and shooters alike. This demand ensures that good examples achieve high prices. Details such as the shape of the hammer make some models more desirable than others, and the collector needs to look closely at every example. Fortunately, the popularity of Mausers has ensured that their history has been well researched, and reference to the books listed in Further Reading will give guidance.

Above

A German 7.65mm pistol, Modell 38H, manufactured by Sauer & Sobn. Approximately 200,000 were made during World War II, and a large number has survived. The design is excellent, and the hammer can be cocked by using the side-mounted lever. Its good design has made it attractive to collectors, but it is still fairly easily available from dealers and at auctions.

Left

Made by Mauser, this is the HSc .32 in pistol. It is a double action weapon, which means that it can be carried safely with a live round in the chamber. For a rapid first shot, the trigger is simply pulled right back and the shot is fired. It is considered risky to carry most self-loading pistols with a round in the chamber, even if there is a safety catch. This model was made between 1939 and the mid-1970s.

*The long-lasting Colt
.45in self-loading pistol
has served the US armed
forces well. First
introduced in 1911
(right), it was modified in
1921, the most obvious
change being the curved
extension at the bottom of
the back of the butt. At
this time it became the
1911A1.*

The US Army, like the military of many other countries, was anxious not to be left behind in re-equipping its forces with self-loading pistols. The Luger had already been rejected, but in 1906 a body was set up to test and decide on the best handgun, and a selection of US, German and British guns were put through some very stringent tests. One by one the pistols were rejected, and in 1907 the Committee reported that the best of the lot were the Colt and the Savage, another US weapon. These two pistols were then subjected to further tests, and in the end the Colt .45in Model of 1911 was selected. It was a good, solid and reliable weapon with a heavy bullet, making it suitable for military service for which stopping power was a major consideration. It served through both world wars as well as in Korea and Vietnam (1965–73), where large numbers were left behind and are now finding their way onto the market. The Colt was replaced as the standard side arm of the US Army in the 1980s by the 9mm Beretta.

Left

The Savage pistol had grooves cut into the slide to offer a good grip when it was pulled back to load the first round. The grips show the Savage trademark – an Indian's head.

Above

One of the competitors in the trials held in the United States to select a self-loading pistol for the Army was a .45 in pistol made by the Savage Arms Company. Although it was not selected, the company produced similar pistols, including this .32 in example. This model was in production between c.1907 and 1926, and it is still, therefore, quite common.

In 1921 some fairly minor modifications were made to the Colt, and the pistol became officially the Model 1911A1. Although nominally called the Colt during World War II, when demand was obviously very heavy, it was manufactured by a number of companies other than Colt, and the frames of these vintage arms will be found bearing names such as Remington Rand and Ithaca. There are other variants, and these are very desirable to collectors, and there is an abundance of published material on the pistols. It is of interest to note that a number of police forces in the USA have recently changed from revolvers to self-loaders, and some have opted for this well-tried and trusted pistol.

The mechanical design of the Colt 1911 was the work of the man who is probably the master designer of firearms, John Moses Browning (1855–1926). His designs have been incorporated in all manner of firearms, ranging from Winchester rifles, through shotguns to self-loading pistols and machine guns. His work on self-loading pistols began in 1889, when he designed one that used, not the recoil principle, but a gas-operated system. By 1895 he had sold the idea to Colt but was looking towards Europe as being a potentially more profitable market.

In 1897 Browning signed an agreement with the Belgian company Fabrique Nationale d'Armes de Guerre in Herstal, and by 1899

Top

The Model 1900 Colt
.38in, which was designed
by John Browning, is a
classic self-loading pistol,
and it is keenly collected.
It was tested by the US
Army, and these tests led
to the development of the
famous 1911 Colt. The
military version of the

Model 1900 was in
production until about
1903, and a sporting
version was made
between 1902 and 1908.
The military versions
bearing US Army marks
are especially sought
after.

Above

John Moses Browning was
one of the most prolific
firearms inventors, and
many pistols are based on
his designs. The model
shown here is a Browning
F-N Model 1906, vest

pocket, six-shot, 6.35mm
pistol. It has a grip safety
catch. It was probably
intended as a self-defence
weapon because the
calibre is small and the
2in (5cm) barrel can

hardly have been
appropriate for shooting
at any great distance. It
was produced in very
large quantities – possibly
as many as a million.

Right

A Modele 1910/22 Pistolet
Automatique Browning,
which was a variant of the
Modele 1910 with a
lengthened barrel. It was
supplied to several
countries, including
Serbia, the Netherlands,
Yugoslavia and Sweden,
and examples will be
found with the markings

of these and other
countries. It is believed
that as many as 750,000
of these pistols were
manufactured, and the
survival rate is high.

Above

A Browning 9mm GP35 pistol, also known as Hi-Power. This weapon was originally produced in Belgium, but during its occupation in World War II a number were made in Canada by John Inglis of Toronto. On this example the original black plastic grips have been replaced by moulded rubber grips for more comfortable shooting.

Left

Designed by a member of the Finnish army, Almo Lahti, this Pistooli L-35 9mm self-loading pistol was adopted by the Finnish forces. This example was probably made about 1944/45. A number were sold commercially and it is a tough, hard-hitting pistol. Most of the Models are made to take a fitted shoulder stock. They are not very common but examples can be found.

the company was producing Browning's pocket pistol. His Modele 1900 of 7.65mm calibre was a great success, and nearly 750,000 were produced. Another of his designs, the Modele 1910, was equally good and was adopted by several European military and police forces. It was modified slightly to meet particular demands, but it was as much in demand as a 7.65mm as a 9mm pistol. This model could be supplied with a 10-shot magazine instead of the normal eight and with a wooden holster, which, like that of the Mauser, also served as a shoulder stock. Browning worked with this firm until his death.

One of his pistols was to see much service during World War II and that was the 9mm Modele 1935-Browning Hi-Power, which saw service with many armed forces, including those of Germany. As in World War I the factory at Liège was occupied by the Germans, who continued production, but the weapons made during the war years are, generally speaking, of a slightly poorer finish. Allied production was continued in Canada by John Inglis of Toronto. After the war the Hi-Power pistol was adopted by several British police forces for specialist firearm units.

In Britain the long-established firm of Webley & Scott also entered the field of self-loaders, producing its first .455in model in 1904. This was not a great success, however, being considered unsafe and dangerous by official testers. After more work, including modifications to the safety catch, the Webley & Scott .455in Self-Loading Mk 1 was officially adopted by the Royal Navy. Two years later it was also accepted for use by the Royal Air Force. Some were tested by the Royal Horse Artillery, and these were fitted with shoulder stocks, but the Artillery decided to retain their revolvers. The Mk 1 pistol was extremely well made, with the typical, rather square look of many Webley self-loaders. A disadvantage was that the machining of the various parts was very critical, and they were, therefore, rather expensive to produce. A smaller version firing a .38in cartridge was produced, and a 9mm pistol using a simpler action was also manufactured.

Above

A French pistol, made by Manufacture d'Armes Automatique de Bayonne and known, in consequence, as the MAB. The model illustrated is a Model D, which was available in .32in or .380in calibre. It was issued to some French military personnel as well as to the German army of occupation. This model and the small Model C may be found with German marks, and these are of especial interest to collectors.

Left

The heavy .455in Webley Self-Loading Mk 1 was adopted by the British Royal Navy in February 1922. It has a grip safety catch, which meant that unless the butt was firmly gripped, the trigger would not operate. It was tested but rejected for general issue by the British Army partly because of this feature, although some were issued to the Royal Horse Artillery. Civilian versions were also available. Despite its rather angular look, this is a reliable weapon, but it was in production for only a limited period, and is not often found.

Later, a small pocket pistol using a .32in cartridge was introduced, and this was the first self-loader to be adopted by the City of London and the Metropolitan Police. To reduce the costs of training, a .22in version was also produced. Many of the .32in and some of the .22in versions, which have short barrels, will be found with the marking MP, indicating that they were official Metropolitan Police weapons.

The advantages of the self-loading pistol were evident to all and many countries began to produce their own models, some using the same system as the Luger while others tried different actions. Bergmanns, for example, used an extremely simple action and were the first that might be called pocket pistols using small cartridges. They had an unusual system of loading the magazine, which was situated in front of the trigger guard and below the barrel, and the cartridges were loaded by swinging a side plate down and laying the cartridges, often in a clip, in the magazine.

One great attraction of self-loaders was the increased firepower they offered, with most magazines holding more than the normal six catridges possible in a revolver. Attempts were made to increase the magazine capacity, and one of the more extreme

Right

Walther, another famous German arms manufacturer, led the world in the design of good quality, double action pistols. This is the Walther Model PP, which was introduced in 1929 and intended primarily for police use. It was first produced in 7.65mm calibre, but its popularity ensured that other calibre models were made.

Left

The Walther PP pistol. Both the PP and the PPK are fairly easily acquired, and they may be found in several calibres. Those with Third Reich markings are especially highly regarded.

Right

The Walther PP was liked by the uniformed police and sundry other units of the Third Reich's forces, but the plain clothes and undercover police wanted a smaller weapon that could be more easily concealed. The result was the PPK, which was essentially a smaller version of the PP and was introduced in 1931. Many of the magazines have a plastic extension on the bottom to give a firmer grip to what is a comparatively small butt.

was the French 7.65mm Pistolet Automatique Union, which had a horse-shoe-shaped magazine holding 35 shots. Self-loaders were, however, more prone to mechanical defects, which often made the weapon inoperable, something the revolver did not usually suffer from. Most self-loaders are fitted with some form of safety catch — some have more than one. The Colt 1911 has, like early Lugers, a grip safety. Others have a magazine safety, which allows the action to function only if there is a magazine in place.

Walther In Germany Mauser continued to produce self-loading pistols, but in 1908 a new name appeared — Walther introduced its first pistol. This was a 6.35mm pistol with a rather chunky appearance, but in 1910 the

firm introduced a larger calibre weapon, the Model 4, which had a calibre of 7.65mm. In 1915 a 9mm model was offered.

The Walther designer made a significant advance in 1929 by introducing the PP pistol, the initials standing for Polizei Pistole. It was the first practical, commercial double action self-loader, and this meant that a round could be loaded into the breech and the hammer lowered with perfect safety. To fire the first shot it was necessary only to pull the trigger. It also had a very efficient and reliable safety catch. The pistol was very popular and was manufactured in a variety of calibres, ranging from .22in up to 9mm. In 1931 a lighter, small version for plain clothes policemen was adopted, and this was the PPK, the K standing for Kriminal.

Below

A Czechoslovakian self-loading pistol, the Praga 7.65mm had a seven-shot magazine. It was first produced in 1920 but was neither popular nor reliable, and apparently only 5,000 were made. The manufacturer, Praga

Zbrojovka, ceased production in 1926. The design is very similar to the Browning 1910 pistol, and the Pragas have little to distinguish them and are not highly sought after.

Above and Left

Two versions of the 9mm Walther Pistole 38 or P38 were developed in 1938, but they were not issued until 1940. The P38 was a replacement for the Luger 08, and it was preferred because it was much easier to manufacture. During World War II some 144,000 were produced, and Walther restarted production in 1957, when the gun was known as the P1. It was official issue to the German Army until 1980, and it was produced in such large numbers that it is still readily available.

Below

The Mannlicher 1901 7.63mm eight-shot pistol was one of the most successful of the early self-loading models and it enjoyed considerable popularity. The magazine was housed in the butt and it was loaded by pushing in the cartridges from a metal strip that was placed in position above the butt. These pistols were soon out of date, however, and the number that has survived is limited. Specialist dealers and auction houses are probably the best sources if you are anxious to obtain an example.

Above

The Spanish company Astra has produced a considerable range of pistols, all of which are of good quality. They were manufactured in a range of calibres – the version of the Model 4000 shown here is 7.65mm, for example – but most use the same mechanical system.

The Luger 08 was a fine pistol, but the Germans found it was rather expensive, partly because it required precise manufacturing techniques, and in 1936 Walther began planning a new 9mm military pistol. The outcome was the P38.

Other well-known names in the firearms industry were Steyr Mannlicher, Dreyse, Glisenti, Beretta and Savage, and all produced a variety of self-loading pistols. Today there is still much happening, and modern technology is being used more and more in the design and production of handguns. Stainless steel has become commonplace, although in general it has proved more successful in revolvers than in self-loaders. Attempts are being made to manufacture caseless cartridges, which would obviously simplify production and reduce costs. Bigger and more powerful cartridges have been developed, and weapons such as the Auto-Mag and Desert Eagle have been used to generate enormous speeds for projectiles. Plastics have been used to make parts of the pistols, and the Glock self-loader has had a big impact on the market. For the dedicated target shooter electronic triggers and super sights, including lasers, have been adapted, requiring new guidelines to be set for some com-

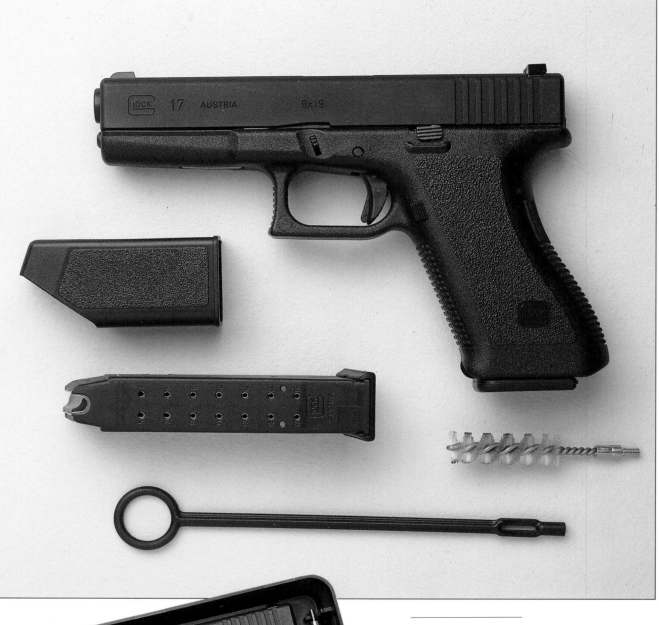

Above and Left

The Austrian-made 9mm Glock 17 pistol was designed by an engineer. It is made from modern plastics and utilizes new mechanical systems and technology. It is supplied as illustrated, with a spare magazine and cleaning gear. The box has a central, tubular hole so that a security chain or cable can be passed through it. It is proving to be a popular weapon.

petitions. Innovations have been made in the shape of target pistols to produce a balanced static firing position, and the butts of some "free" pistols are so complex that the gun is worn rather like a glove. Magazine capacities have been upgraded, and now a pistol will hold 12–15 rounds with ease.

There have been experiments in replacing powder as the propellant. The Gyrojet pistol, for example, used what was, in effect, a small rocket in place of the conventional bullet, but it was not a great success. Bullets have been altered to reduce the chances of ricochets in urban police work, while others have been produced to develop maximum stopping power at low velocities. There have been attempts to introduce slightly unusual calibres, but the old favourites seem to prevail.

Above

A 9mm SIG Model 210–6, this Swiss-made gun is one of the finest and best made self-loading pistols available. It is solid and reliable, and is valued by shooters for its consistent accuracy. Although it is expensive, it is reckoned to be worth the high cost.

Left

One of the new Colt self-loading pistols, the Mark IV/70 Government .45in automatic calibre is essentially a top quality version of the standard 1911A1. In addition to the .45in version seen here, the gun is also available in 9mm and .38in Super calibres. It is produced especially for accuracy in competition shooting, and the barrels are made specifically with this in mind.

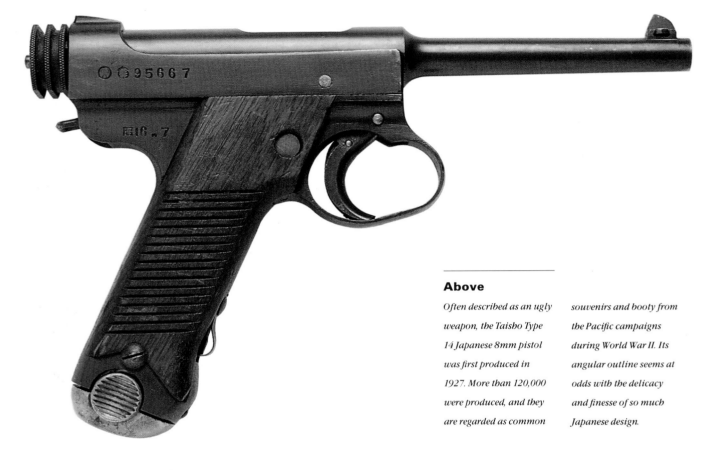

Above

Often described as an ugly weapon, the Taisho Type 14 Japanese 8mm pistol was first produced in 1927. More than 120,000 were produced, and they are regarded as common souvenirs and booty from the Pacific campaigns during World War II. Its angular outline seems at odds with the delicacy and finesse of so much Japanese design.

Right

One very well known name in the world of guns is that of Beretta whose Italian factories produce sporting guns of top quality, as well as military pistols. This Model 1951 E is one of a contract to supply Egypt. This firm now supplies the United States with their standard 9mm sidearm.

Accessories can be an excellent area for collectors since hardly any require any form of licence to hold and most are comparatively inexpensive. Because the purpose of many of these pieces is not immediately apparent, they are often overlooked by the casual buyer. Junk shops and odds-and-end boxes are worthwhile hunting grounds, especially for reloading items, whose function is often obscure.

Loading Equipment Loading early handguns required quite a number of items, compared with modern weapons with breech-loading metal cartridges. The percussion revolver used gunpowder, which was normally carried in a metal powder flask. The number of different styles, patterns and designs of flasks was considerable, but in general the metal flask supplied with a percussion revolver was reasonably standard. It was usually smooth and slightly pear-shaped. The upper section – the charger – was of brass and could be unscrewed to allow easy

refilling. The base of the charger has an internal spring-operated cut-off, and the nozzle normally incorporated some method of altering the measure of powder deposited. This was done by adjusting the length of the charger, the size of the charge being indicated by means of a graduated slot cut into the neck.

The charge of powder was measured by placing the finger over the top of the cylindrical charger, pressing open the spring to operate the cut-off and inverting the flask. This allowed the powder to run out of the body and fill the tubular charger. The cut-off was then released, locking just the correct quantity of powder in the charger so that the flask could be turned back up. The nozzle of the charger was placed over a chamber in the cylinder and the powder poured in. A bullet was then placed in the mouth of the chamber and forced down onto the powder using either the ram fitted to the revolver or a separate one.

Left

A Mauser HSc 7.65mm. Production of these models began c1940 and they were issued to the German Luftwaffe and Wehrmacht. It is a double action weapon and could be carried with a round loaded in the chamber with perfect safety. Production numbers were high and the gun is still common.

Above

The Bergmann pistol with the magazine cover partially opened and the hammer cocked.

The name of the manufacturer is often engraved around the top of the flask, and the great majority will be found to be by one of two British manufacturers, Dixon or Hawksley. Some of the older flasks were embossed with designs, and those supplied with the early Colt revolvers are sought after. So popular are they that modern copies have been produced, so care is needed when buying such pieces.

Other essential components for early revolvers were the percussion caps, and these were supplied in paper or cloth packets or in round tins, which were often japanned (varnished) to prevent rusting. Some tins have a printed label bearing the supplier's name, and others have the name simply impressed on the lid.

The last essential was a bullet mould, for supplies of ready-made bullets were uncommon in much of the world of the 19th century and it was necessary to be able to cast one's own. The moulds vary considerably, but most are of a scissors pattern and open to allow removal of the cast bullet. Most were designed to cast two bullets with each filling, one bullet usually being round and the other cylindro-conical. Many moulds are stamped with the maker's name, while others carry either the calibre or the bore of the bullet.

All of these items appear on the market from time to time, and each is collected in its own right. The more ordinary ones are more common and normally sell for around £100/$150. Moulds are popular and can often be ascribed to various revolvers, when they are very collectable. Like the powder flasks, some of the more popular sizes of moulds have been reproduced, although many are clearly marked "Made in Italy" and are unlikely to deceive a collector. Cap tins are little regarded and should be available for very small sums.

These three items were the essentials, but there were extras such as a small wrench to unscrew the nipples, which were rather vulnerable to damage. A small turned wooden or ivory box containing a set of spare nipples was often supplied. A cleaning rod was also commonly available, and tins of wax lubricant were often included in the case. Small tools such as turnscrews were also supplied with some weapons.

The introduction of pinfire and centrefire cartridges was a big step forward, but it did create its own problems, for the cartridge cases were a little more complex and reloading more difficult. However, the makers soon produced various tools for the job, and these are not uncommon and are generally undervalued, largely because few collectors rec-

Above

This magazine holder for a Government Colt 1911 dates from 1918 and carries the manufacturer's title. World War II examples are fairly common, but early examples like this are less often seen.

ognize their purpose. Some of the best sources of information are the old gun shop catalogues, many of which have been re-printed and illustrate these tools.

Cases Many of these early percussion weapons were sold in wooden cases, commonly made of oak or mahogany. They were lined with green baize or similar material and were fitted with a lock or hooked catches. The inside of the lid frequently carried a printed label giving the supplier's or manu-facturer's name and instructions on the use of the weapon. The various items were placed in compartments marked out with thin wooden dividers. The style of casing varied

— the layout for Colt revolvers manufactured in Britain, for example, differs from those of American construction. European cases often have inside compartments that were specifi-cally contoured to accommodate and save each accessory, top quality cases are covered in moulded leather. Some early Smith & Wesson Model 1 revolvers were sold in presentation cases of moulded gutta-percha with the lids embossed with a revolver or a stand of flags, although the company later reverted to more conventional wooden cases. Some cases had brass plaques on the lid bearing the owner's name and sometimes a coat of arms, which means that the original owner can often be traced. Any such details

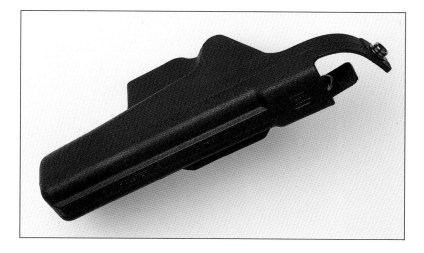

Above

Light, durable and easy to produce in quantity, this modern belt holster of moulded plastic is for the Glock 17 pistol. The flap at the top holds the pistol firmly in place but may be easily flipped open with the thumb.

greatly enhance the value of the cased set, and the better known the owner the greater the value.

The adoption of pinfire, rimfire and centre fire weapons led to a reduction in the number of essential accessories. Cases for centre fire and pinfire weapons were commonly of leather in the style of a small attaché case with carrying handle and straps. The lining was of varied colours and, in addition to the

revolver, the case normally contained an oil bottle, a cleaning brush and rod, and a tray for holding a number of cartridges. Other less common accessories found in a few cases are special small cleaning tools and tools for adjusting sights.

Cheaper revolvers from the late 19th and early 20th century were often sold in cardboard boxes with, perhaps, a partition or two and details of the weapon or its use printed on the inside lid. Although these are less attractive than the wooden or leather cases, they are of interest. Modern handguns are also sold in mass-produced cardboard boxes or, for some better quality models, wooden boxes, but these are but poor imitations of their ancestors.

Cases are eagerly sought after by collectors and dealers, for the value of any handgun is enhanced if it is in a case. It is often difficult to tell if weapon and case belong to each other, although tight or awkward fit may suggest that something is not quite right. Any case in good condition will sell well.

Above

Few revolvers were fitted with any form of safety catch, but this Webley W.P. 320 was an exception. A small bar set at the top of the frame could be pushed back to lock the hammer in such a way that it could

not be cocked. The hammer was shrouded to reduce the chances of its being caught or snagged on clothing, and it also lacked a firing pin, which was mounted in the frame.

Right

Another smaller company is that of Jennings of California, USA, who produce a selection of pistols including a little .22in pocket pistol.

Below

Essentially a Colt .45in pistol, this version is actually produced by Auto-Ordnance. It is available in a variety of calibres. The trigger pull, very important in competition shooting, can be adjusted to suit the shooter.

Holsters Because the handgun was normally carried for personal protection it needed to be readily accessible. The usual method of achieving this was by means of a belt holster, and there is an enormous variety of these. The earlier ones are obviously rarer, and those carried in the USA are probably the most eagerly collected. Not only do they have a more romantic association but their designs are so varied.

The usual European military holsters are fairly standard and conform to a similar pattern, although they did vary according to models. They are of leather and have a flap. Those made for self-loading weapons often feature a compartment to hold a spare magazine or, in the case of revolvers, a fitting to accommodate a cleaning rod or a few extra rounds. Shapes obviously vary since the holsters were designed for specific models, but some such as the Luger have extra fittings to hold the detachable shoulder board, which could be fitted to the butt to convert the weapon into a carbine. The Mauser Broomhandle pistol was supplied in a wooden hol-

Above

One of the best known holsters is the one that was used for the Luger '08 pistol. This example, from 1917, still retains a spare magazine in the compartment at the front. Inside the top flap is a pocket containing a small tool that serves as a screwdriver and a device to assist in loading the magazine.

Below

A rig for a Navy Colt percussion revolver – a holster, cartridge pouch and belt dating from the Civil War period; the holster has been modified by the removal of the top fold-over flap. A black leather Slim Jim holster with incised decoration; the black strap is marked

with the name "Friend & Bro" and it was made c.1885. A similar brown leather holster, but made to be carried on the left or on the right side with butt of the revolver pointing forwards. Genuine early holsters are not found often, but reproductions are quite common.

Left

The material used for military belts and straps is known as webbing, and this dark blue holster and belt are, except for the colour, the same as the standard military issue. The colour indicates that they were just for use by the London Metropolitan Police on the rare occasions when they were issued with firearms.

Right

An official-issue brown leather holster for the Colt revolver. It is dated 1917 and was made by G. & K, and the owner's name, "Wm. J.T. 305 T.M.B.", is marked on the belt loop. There is a small brass ring at the bottom for securing a thong to the thigh. A brown leather holster with carved decoration for a Colt Single Action Army Revolver. The back flap is marked "407X 4471/2" and probably dates from c.1900. A plain brown leather holster, probably made for a short-barrelled Colt revolver, and also dating from c.1900. Original holsters with any claim to being antique are not common, but they may sometimes be found at fairs and conventions.

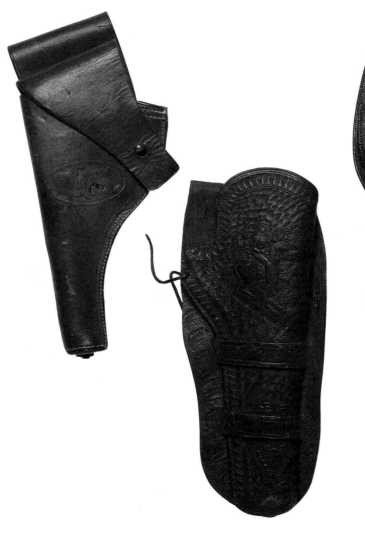

ster, which also served as detachable shoulder stock. Leather was often replaced by woven materials, and webbing magazine holders and holsters were commonly used during World War II. Various patterns of these webbing holsters were produced for different branches of the forces.

Gunbelts vary from the very ordinary, everyday type to elaborate, silver-encrusted ones, although such examples were usually for show rather than use. The standard British officer's belt was the wide, leather type with brass fittings designed originally by General Sir Samuel J. Browne (1824–1901). The holster could be attached in various ways, but the most usual was by means of loops through which the belt was passed. A few holsters, however, were attached with brass spring clips. Many European armies copied the Sam Browne belt with its cross straps and other fittings.

The belts worn by other ranks were usually of a plain, basic design and of leather or webbing, but the buckle will sometimes give information as to nationality. The holster and belt often carry inspection or manufacturer's dates, and a check of the inside and back of the holster is always useful.

Early American holsters were primarily designed for the cavalry, and because of the length of the barrel of the Colt revolver they were long and narrow – hence their nickname, Slim Jims. These had a flap, which folded over to cover the butt, and they were worn with the butt pointing to the front, which meant that the wrist had to be turned when drawing the weapon. It was not until 1905 that US holsters were altered so that the butt pointed to the rear.

Civilian holsters were more varied, although many suppliers offered the military styles. Holsters from eastern Europe, Mexico and the Frontier period of America were often decorated with brass studs, embroidery or applied materials. The Western holster was often made locally and varied between the plain and totally functional to those with fine, decorative carving. Many were made

by using a long piece of leather for the back part, which was folded over before two sets of cuts were made to create two loops. The front section, which held the gun, was then folded over and slipped through the two slots. This was a simple process and meant that the holster could fit any width of belt.

Most Western holsters feature a small loop of leather thong at the top, which slipped over the spur of the hammer to hold the gun safely in place while the wearer was bouncing along on a horse or mounting and dismounting. Some also featured a leather thong hanging from the base, and this was used to secure the holster firmly to the thigh, partly to prevent it flapping about and also to prevent it riding up when the gun, which was a rather tight fit in the holster, was drawn. The

Above

A black leather holster suitable for a small automatic pistol such as a Webley .32in; it was made by William Jenkinson & Co. Ltd and was fitted with a pocket for a spare magazine. A webbing holster for the 9mm Hi-Power Browning pistol, dated 1965; it has inside pockets for a spare magazine and cleaning rod. A Canadian khaki holster made for the Browning Hi-Power pistol and dated 1944; it has an inside metal

compartment for a spare magazine and a pocket for a cleaning rod. Objects such as these can often be found at army surplus stores.

Right

The German-made Mauser Broomhandle pistol with standard fittings, including a fine set of leather attachments to hold the wooden holster. The leather has a fitting to hold a cleaning rod as well as a compartment to hold a spare magazine spring.

same system was continued through to modern US holsters, although it seems seldom to have been used. The double holster of the two-gun hero of the cinema was rare and not often carried in real life.

These patterns of holster remained popular, although as pistol shooting developed as a sport and law enforcement turned more to handguns, holster design developed until today the choice is very wide. Some are made with an open front so that when the weapon is drawn it is pulled forwards, rather than up and forwards as in the older style. This is designed to save that split second of time on a fast draw that might be crucial in an emergency or tight competition. Others are designed to hold the weapon at a particular angle or to pivot when the wearer sits down. Some are lined with soft leather to reduce wear on the gun and to facilitate quick drawing, and others are reduced to the absolute minimum leather necessary to hold the gun in place. Many of the older gunbelts were fitted with a series of loops to hold cartridges firmly but ready to hand and some modern belts still use this system. Modern police belts sometimes have cartridge loops, but various fittings can also hold handcuffs, Mace, keys, torches, batons, spare magazines or speed loaders.

In addition to the visible holster, there are numerous versions designed to carry the weapon in an unobtrusive way. The most common is the shoulder holster. Although primarily a civilian accessory, shoulder holsters were used by some military personnel – air crews, for example – and there are several patterns of these. In addition to a variety of shoulder holsters, there are ankle holsters, handbag holsters and even holsters for carrying sub-machine guns and sawn-off shot guns.

Large numbers of these holsters are available commercially, but the earlier and less common military ones are seldom expensive and can often be found in sales of war surplus material and similar venues.

Left

A US military shoulder holster, the Caliber .45 M7, which was developed during World War II. It was a modified version of the earlier M3 holster, which was changed after tests were carried out by various service boards. Shoulder holsters are most appropriate when the wearer wears special clothing or extra accessories.

Left

A shoulder holster designed to let the weapon hang horizontally. The straps cross the shoulders at the back and the double loop is secured to the waist belt to ensure a firm fit. The leather holster is moulded to fit a particular weapon – in this case a replica Colt .45 in pistol.

Right

One of the few drawbacks to the revolver is the difficulty of rapid loading, and various systems were devised to overcome this problem. The round gadget seen here is a speed loader, *which was designed to drop six rounds into the cylinder in one movement. The speed strips were made to hold six rounds, which could be rapidly stripped off in the chambers.*

Loaders

Speed loaders are designed to overcome the weakness of revolvers, which is the time taken to reload. Attempts were made to find a way of loading the cylinder with all six or five cartridges in one go. One of the early models was designed by a British Army officer, William Prideaux, and it was used by the British Army from 1918 until 1926. It consisted of a metal frame into which the cartridges were pushed, and when the revolver was loaded it was carefully positioned above the cylinder so that the bullets were above the chambers and then pressed down. This action caused the loader to release the cartridges, which fell into the chambers. The basic principle has continued, although it has varied in detail. Prideaux loaders are not common and, together with the all-leather holster, sell for £150–200/$225–300. Other styles

Above

Designed by William Prideaux in 1914 this rapid loader saw service during World War I. It was carried in a leather pouch on the officer's Sam Browne belt. It held six cartridges and was placed on the cylinder and pressed down dropping all six cartridges in the chambers.

Above

The example on the left is a commercial Prideaux loader while the right one is an official issue dated *1919. These are not common and now sell at around £100–150/$150–225 each.*

Right

Modern box of practice ammunition. Both case and projectile are of plastic and would be used for training when it would be dangerous or impossible to use conventional ammunition.

of speed loaders included a rubber strip to hold the cartridges which was stripped off after the cartridges were in the chamber.

Another development to increase firepower was the extended magazine, which could hold more rounds than the standard pattern. Most hold about 20 rounds and extend below the bottom of the butt, but one designed for the 1911 Colt self-loader held many more and was so long that it was carried in a special case attached to the belt. The capacity meant that the Colt's rate of fire almost equalled that of a machine pistol. One distinctive form holding 32 rounds was developed for the Luger, and, because of its shape, it is known as the snail drum. These are rare and much sought after by collectors and so are expensive items.

Above

Speed loaders for modern revolvers.

Above

Box of vintage .22in ammunition.

Right

For minimum friction between gun and leather, the leather of this shoulder holster has been reduced to a simple skeleton.

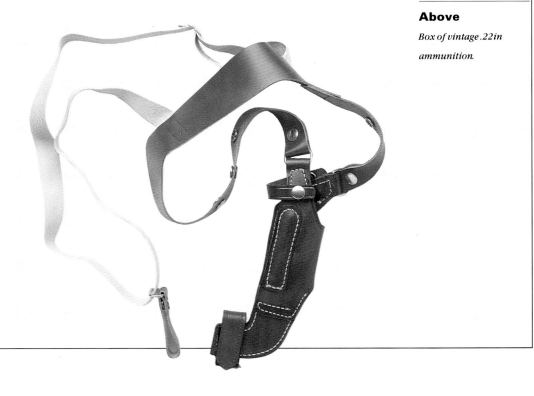

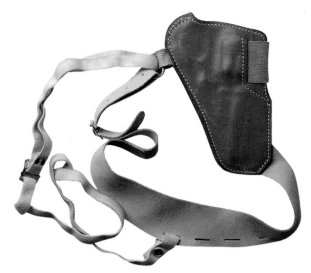

Left

This type of shoulder holster allows the revolver to hang with the butt down. To draw it, the weapon is simply pulled downwards.

Left Below

An unusual and mysterious loader for a revolver, this one holds six rounds and is hinged at the centre. It has a ring side fitting which bears the legend Revolver Cartridge Clip Corp New York./38/Pat Pending. This is an example of the odd accessory that suddenly appears and stimulates interest.

Lanyards Another small accessory that is of interest is the lanyard. Descended from the sword knot, this is a cord or leather thong, which normally attaches to the butt of the gun. The other end circles either the neck or the shoulder and makes sure that if the gun is dropped it will not be lost. Many simply loop through a lanyard ring fitted at the base of the butt, but others are fastened to the ring by means of a spring clip. Obviously they are fairly basic, but there are a number of variants, and in the British armed forces the colour varies with the services – khaki for the Army and light blue for the Royal Air Force. This variation applies also to the webbing holsters and belts, and dark blue patterns were issued for the rare occasions when the British police carried revolvers. Searching for these various bits and pieces can occupy quite a lot of time and effort, but the pleasure afforded by a find more than compensates for the trouble taken.

Right

A lanyard fitted to the British Army Enfield revolver. The securing cords were supplied in appropriate colours – khaki for the Army, light blue for the Royal Air Force and white for the Military Police. The other end of the cord was either secured to the shoulder or worn around the neck.

5

Ammunition

No matter how magnificent a firearm may be, it is useless if there is no ammunition. One of the greatest drawbacks to almost every early form of firearm was the fact that after the shot had been fired the weapon was useful only as a bludgeon. At best, loading was a slow business, and the use of a powder flask, priming powder and a bullet involved a considerable number of movements. Attempts to speed up loading were made from the earliest days, and one of the first was a wooden or horn container that held just one charge of powder. Twelve were suspended from a belt or bandoleer, worn over one shoulder and across the chest.

For the military speed of reloading could be vital, and paper cartridges were developed. A strip of thick paper was rolled around a wooden former to make a tube, and one end was closed by twisting the paper. A charge of powder was poured in, a ball placed on top and the other end closed by another twist. Each soldier carried a supply of these paper cartridges in some form of pouch. The cartridges were a little vulnerable, so they were sometimes carried in wooden blocks drilled with holes to accommodate each cartridge. To load his musket or pistol the soldier bit off one twisted end, poured a pinch of powder into the pan and then tipped the rest down the barrel, adding the paper at the end to serve as a wad. He then rammed down the bullet using the ramrod, and the weapon was loaded. Similar cartridges were made for the percussion revolvers, but these often had a small tag made of material that could be pulled to split open the paper.

A few handguns were produced that did not need the paper to be torn, for the cartridge contained not only the powder but also enclosed a small capsule of percussive compound. The cartridge was loaded into the breech of the gun and the detonation was achieved by a long, thin needle, which was punched forward to puncture the paper, hit the percussive pellet and so fire the charge. Their success was limited and few examples of the cartridges have survived.

Right

This Austrian-made self-loading pistol is about 4¹/₂in (11cm) long, and it is known, appropriately, as Little Tom. This model is of .25in calibre, but a larger .32in calibre version was also produced. It is unusual in that it is a double action pistol – once it is loaded and cocked, the hammer can be lowered and need only be pressed to fire the first shot.

With the advent of the percussion system there arose the need to fit small caps onto small nipples, and in bad weather or with cold fingers this was an irksome task. To speed up and simplify matters cap dispensers were designed. These are commonly of two types – either a flat disc or a long, rectangular bar. Both incorporate a spring, which is compressed as it is loaded with caps, and the open end has a spring that retains the last cap over an opening. To cap a chamber or the breech of a rifle, the exposed cap is pressed on the nipple and the dispenser pulled clear. The retaining spring allows the next cap to move along and then grips it ready for the next loading.

From the earliest times there were numerous attempts to overcome the serious limitation of having only a single shot, and the most popular and simple was the double-barrelled weapon. Some had the barrels mounted side by side and others one on top of the other. The principle was extended to three- and four-barrelled weapons, but even this system was comparatively slow because of the steps that were necessary before each shot could be fired.

Another solution was the super-imposed load technique. The barrel was made with two touchholes, and the first charge of powder and ball was poured down the barrel so that it was adjacent to the rear touchhole.

Left

The Lilliput, which was produced in Germany in the late 1920s, is so small that it is really more of a model than a real weapon. Its size alone makes it something of a collector's piece, and examples are not common. The Kolibri, which was made in Austria, is even smaller at only 3mm calibre. The tiny centrefire cartridges are also keenly collected.

Below

These mid-19th-century paper cartridges were manufactured by Eley Brothers, the famous London ammunition firm. The tape projecting from the tip of each was designed to facilitate the tearing of the paper to release the gunpowder. The smaller cartridges were for the .31in Pocket Colt percussion revolver, and others were made for the Adams .45in revolver. The largest of the examples shown here is a 15 gauge, with a calibre of .68in. The fragility of these cartridges made it unlikely that they will survive, and they are not common.

Right

The open cylinder of a Colt Python .357in Magnum revolver. The famous trademark, a small horse, can be seen on the frame.

Left

These lead bullets were made for 19th-century percussion revolvers. Some weapons were still using spherical bullets, but the cylindro-conical types were becoming more common. Many bullets were cast with "tails", to which were fitted the wads that were meant to ensure that they fitted tightly inside the barrel. Other bullets were made with a cannelure or channel around the base, which was filled with lubricating grease. Examples of these early bullets are fairly common, and they may be cast from original moulds.

A substantial wad was then located in front of the bullet and the second charge poured down, which was then next to the front touchhole. By various ingenious arrangements of the ignition system the front charge was fired first, followed by the rear charge, a system that gave a reasonably rapid two-shot capability. The loading and sequence of firing was obviously vital, and should the rear charge be fired first or both shots fired together there was likely to be a nasty accident.

Matchlock, wheel-lock, and flintlock revolvers were only a limited success, for the ignition system was mechanically difficult and awkward to design. It was the advent of the percussion system and, ultimately, the percussion cap that opened the door to a cure for the problem. The cap first made possible pepperbox revolvers and then, in the middle of the 19th century, the percussion revolver. These new weapons gave a firepower of a usual six shots and with some rather cumbersome pinfire revolvers as many as 30 or more shots. Nevertheless, despite the great advance in weapon technology, the percussion revolver and, to a much lesser degree, the pinfire revolver were still rather slow in loading. The final breakthrough was the development of the centre fire, metal-cased cartridge in the 1860s, and the old slow muzzle-loading system was replaced by the easier breech-loading weapons.

Breech-loading was not new – attempts had been made from the earliest days of firearms to use it. Early cannon were mostly breech-loading, but these and later systems all suffered from one great problem – leakage of gas. In order to load at the breech some means of access was obviously necessary, but to achieve this there had to be some sort of opening. It was easy enough to devise this, but the problem was to make certain that when the charge was ignited the breech was sealed to ensure that all the gases generated expanded along the barrel to propel the missile with maximum force. It was also important to prevent leakage to protect the operator from the unpleasant effects of flame and smoke that were blown out through gaps around the breech.

As early as 1812 the Swiss inventor Johannes Pauly had designed a centrefire cartridge with a brass base and a cardboard body just like the modern shotgun cartridge. Pauly's guns had drop-down barrels, and the cartridge was loaded into the breech in exactly the same way as modern shotguns. Despite its obvious advantages the system was not adopted and faded away, and specimens of the Pauly cartridge are rare.

Left

This plated and engraved .380in Star self-loading pistol was made in Spain. The company has produced large numbers of a wide range of firearms, most of which are in the lower price range. Several similar pistols but in different calibres were produced by during the 1930s and 1940s.

There were numerous attempts to produce breech-loading rifles and carbines, but the handgun remained basically a paper cartridge, muzzle-loading weapon until the invention of the Smith & Wesson rimfire cartridge. The wall of the rim of the case had to be thin so that the hammer could crush it and detonate the fulminate deposted internally. The thin metal base had a habit of bulging slightly under the internal pressure that developed as the powder burnt, and the bulged cases could and did jam the cylinder of the revolver. The other great disadvantage of the rimfire cartridge was that it could not be reloaded for it was beyond the capability of the individual to deposit a thin layer of fulminate inside the rim. The US master patent held by Smith & Wesson prevented most other makers from using loading systems that inserted the charge from the rear, and they produced a variety of ingenious and sometimes impractical ideas to circumvent the limitation, until the master patent expired in 1873.

In Britain the patent taken out by Colonel Edward Boxer in January 1866 changed the military cartridge for the British Army. The metal case, fashioned from thin brass sheet, was rolled around a metal former and then fitted to a base containing the primer. As a shot was fired the metal case expanded, effectively sealing the breech. The Boxer cartridge was primarily for rifles, but a .577in cartridge was produced for the Webley revolver. A .442in Boxer cartridge was also produced for the Royal Irish Constabulary revolver made by Webley in 1868. In the same year the converted Adams percussion revolver was officially adopted as the standard revolver for the British Army, and its .455in cartridge was a form of Boxer with a brass body and iron cup with the primer. It held 13 grains of black powder and a lead bullet with a hollow base, which was intended to concentrate the gases propelling it from the barrel.

The last step towards the current handgun cartridge was the introduction of a drawn brass case in place of the brass foil one, which tended to become separated from the base and jam the weapon. Because the handgun cartridge was much shorter than that of the rifle, it was easier and cheaper to produce a drawn brass case.

In the USA in 1873 a whole range of metal-cased cartridges was tested at the Frankford Arsenal, Philadelphia, and the end result was the development of an almost universal type of cartridge with a drawn brass case and a lead bullet. The only real difference between most US and British cartridges

lay in the fitting of the cap. While the vast majority of British cases used the Boxer system, many US ones used a Berdan primer. Externally there is no apparent difference, but internally the Boxer cartridge has one central hole through the base leading to the cap, while the Berdan cartridge uses two small holes and a slightly different style of fitting.

The development of the breech-loading system led to a growth of interest in shooting. Sport, law enforcement, military, hunting and self-defence interests all felt that they needed a special type of gun and, as often as not, a special cartridge. Expense was one consideration, but range and the ability to stop a charging animal or criminal were all factors that encouraged manufacturers to produce numerous cartridges. While the basic shape of the cartridges was similar, the sizes were very varied.

The method of describing cartridges became complex and it is still so today, with no generally accepted universal practice. In general, the diameter or calibre of the bullet is expressed in inches – .45in, .38in or .22in, for example. In Europe, on the other hand, measurements are in millimetres, 9mm being the most common. However, some car-

tridges also have a second figure, and this may refer to the case length or to the powder charge. A black powder cartridge described as a .45–60 would mean that the bullet was .45in calibre and the black powder charge was 60 grains. Some cartridges are described with calibre and the name of the weapon for which it was made – 9mm Steyr, for instance.

Calibre is a matter of choice, but in general indoor target shooters favour the .22in cartridge, for it is cheap and there is little recoil, making it easy to shoot a large number of rounds without discomfort. Since most indoor small bore target shooting is done at no more than 25 yards (23m), the powder charge and bullet need be only small. The .22in cartridge is also popular for small game shooting. There are two sizes of this popular calibre, .22in LR (long rifle) and .22in Short. Despite its name, the .22 LR is a popular pistol and revolver round, while .22in Short is preferred for rapid fire because the slide has a shorter distance to travel when extracting the case and the gun can then fire fractionally faster.

Military cartridges tend to be larger and more powerful, and the popular calibres range from 9mm to .455in. Police calibres are about the same, whereas weapons for

Below

This fine quality weapon is a Hammerli International .22in target pistol. The long barrel helps to increase accuracy, and the wooden grips are contoured for a firm, comfortable hold. Top class shooters often have the butt grips specially moulded to fit their hand exactly. Some top grade target pistols fetch extremely high prices.

Opposite Below

A rare collector's box of 7.65mm Mauser ammunition. This would be welcome to a collector as it is complete and unopened.

self-defence, which are intended primarily for short-range shooting, usually use calibres of around .25in, .32in or perhaps .38in. In the 1930s there was a move to increase the powder charge to give the bullet more speed and power, and the so-called Magnum cartridge was introduced. Since the diameter of the bullets is about the same, the Magnum cases are made slightly longer than the normal cartridge so that they cannot be loaded into weapons not designed to take Magnum loads. There have been attempts to introduce what might be called non-standard calibres such as .41in, and persuasive arguments have been put forward to suggest that it would be a useful round for the police with its strong stopping power.

The smallest self-loading handgun — or should it be finger gun — was the Kolibri, which used a 2.7mm centrefire cartridge with a 3 grain bullet.

The other variable feature of cartridges is the shape of the case. In general, those used in revolvers have a rim like the first Smith & Wesson ones. Those made for self-loading pistols do not usually have a rim, but they do have a groove around the base so that the extractor can hook onto the empty case; these cases are known as rimless. Most

handgun cartridges are straight-sided, but some — like the Japanese Nambu 8mm, for example — have a shoulder or bottleneck, and that part of the case holding the bullet is narrower than the rest. The .30in Luger is the same shape, the object being to have a main section with a larger powder capacity while keeping the bullet size the same. Some modern revolvers, such as the French-made Manurhin, use a similar cartridge to develop an enormous velocity for the .22in bullet.

Over the past few years there has been a growing interest in long-distance pistol shooting, and special pistols, such as the Contender, have been developed. However, these might be described as hand rifles, for they are designed to fire a rifle cartridge.

The great feature about collecting cartridges is that identification is usually fairly simple. The base of the cartridge normally bears some stamped marks, which may be a name or numbers. These head stamps as they are called will often provide the details of where and when the cartridge was made, and most have been identified and published lists are available.

Cartridges should always be treated with respect for they are potentially lethal. It is

Above

Two versions of the Smith & Wesson Model 27 .357in Magnum revolver. The example with the 6in (15cm) barrel is designed primarily for target work, and it is fitted with special grips. The version with the 3½in (9cm) barrel is fitted with wooden, contoured grips. Such short-barrelled revolvers, sometimes called "snubbies", are often used when concealment is important.

Ammunition and the Law

In most countries legislation governing the possession of ammunition exists, and it is as well to check the local laws. In some European countries certain types of cartridges are prohibited, even though they are of a common calibre. Their distinguishing feature is the type of missile fitted to the cartridge – some bullets were designed so that the head would expand when the target was hit, while others were fitted with steel cores so that they would pierce armour. These are now prohibited under the European Community regulations, but it is possible for a collector to be granted permission to acquire them.

Below

Some modern ammunition. The silver cartridge at the top is dummy 9mm round and the black bullets are coated with a nylon compound designed to cut down on lead pollution from the bullet. The copper-coloured bullets are full jacketed 9mm and .45in bullets. There is a .22in short and a .22in long rifle cartridge.

possible to acquire inert cartridges from which the charge has been withdrawn and the primer "killed". However, it is impossible to know if the cartridge is live or inert just by looking at it, and it is wise to treat all cartridges as if they were live. Fired cases are occasionally fitted with new bullets, and these may be recognized by the fact that the primer will be dented at the centre where it has been struck by the hammer.

There are several ways to display the cartridges. Corrugated panels are available, and these are useful when the display is likely to be modified and cases moved around. For more permanent displays it is possible to secure each case with a loop of thread or fine wire around the case and through a covered backing board. Another system is to purchase plastic cases, which are divided up into a number of compartments, each of which can hold one specimen. This is, in many respects, the best method, for the cartridge is unaffected and can be removed for examination at any time, while full details of the specimen can be recorded on a label in each compartment. Alternatively, the details may be written on the case with a fine-tipped spirit pen.

Associated with the cartridges are the boxes and packs in which they were sold. The tins in which unusual calibres, such as the Kolibri, were supplied are eagerly sought after and greatly valued by collectors.

Listed in Further Reading are several books that deal with cartridges, including some that list most usual types together with their dimensions and a brief history of the round. Most cartridges are inexpensive, and there are organizations dedicated to the collecting of ammunition, so the opportunities to build up a collection are ready and waiting. They also have the great advantage for those with limited space – they do not take up a lot of room.

Shooting and guns have always proved attractive subjects for writers, and printers have been kept busy supplying a wide range of printed material in addition to books. For those with an interest in guns there is a wide range of peripheral – often paper – material, usually known as ephemera, just waiting to be collected.

Much ephemera is very fragile and liable to destruction, but some, such as old catalogues, is a little more durable. During the later part of the 19th century most gunsmiths offered an extremely wide range of items for the shooter, and they issued catalogues that were often well printed. These are mines of information, and those produced by some of the larger firms are almost textbooks of contemporary firearms. Most are well illustrated and often include brief explanations of the products. It is an interesting, if somewhat depressing, pastime to look at prices and compare them with current ones. Obviously it is much more interesting if the genuine article can be found, but modern reprints of the old catalogues should not be disregarded for they contain a wealth of detail.

Gunmakers also advertised fairly widely, and it is always worthwhile scanning contemporary newspapers or magazines for such insertions. Ideally, the page with the advertisement on it should be kept intact, but such are the pressures on living space that it may be necessary to clip them. If this is done it is vital to note the source, including the name of newspaper and, most importantly, the date. Some of the bigger manufacturers and suppliers often rose to special occasions and distributed leaflets to encourage sales or warn of problems, but these are fairly rare as their working life was very short.

Trade cards are another rare item, for by their nature they were give-away, throwaway items. Nevertheless, odd ones still survive and turn up at ephemera fairs. The trade labels that were stuck inside cases are seldom found apart from the cases, but some collectors in the past unwisely removed them and they may very occasionally appear. A number of these labels have been copied and suitably aged and distressed and they may fool the enthusiast, but a close look at the texture of the print with a small lens will probably enable a decision on authenticity to be made.

Right

From left to right: A US Secret Service instruction book for Smith & Wesson revolvers; a children's guide to pistols published in Britain in 1966; a popular instruction book, dating from c.1920; an official British War Office instruction book dating from 1937 on the .38in pistol; a Colt publicity booklet, based on a reprint of an article by A. Lane, World Champion Pistol Shot c.1914; an invaluable modern reference book, which was published in Texas and which lists details of all Browning-designed firearms.

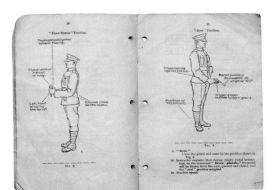

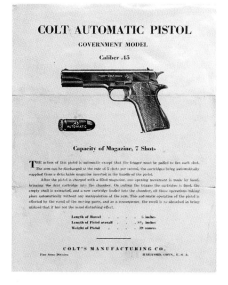

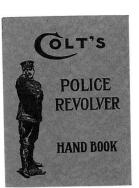

Left and Below

From left to right: A leaflet for the Colt 1911A1, which was supplied with the weapon on purchase; it is undated but must post-date 1921, when the design was altered. A 24-page promotional booklet for the police, dated 1913; it contains instructions on the use and care of the Colt revolver. A folding booklet for the Colt 1911 automatic pistol; the booklet pre-dates 1921. Early examples of this type of leaflet are fairly rare, and they are seldom seen in such good condition as these.

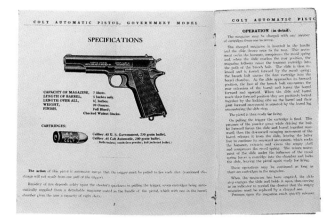

Interest in things military and shooting seems to have been much more widespread in the later part of the 19th century and the early years of the 20th century. Many magazines and newspapers carried articles on the latest developments in the arms field, and these are worth seeking out in contemporary publications.

One way of storing these fragile items is in transparent plastic envelopes, which can be purchased in a variety of sizes either loose or in folders, in which the papers are held flat and may be read without touching them. Always store paper ephemera flat and in a dry place, and keep away from direct sunlight.

As prices and costs began to mount, the older mahogany and oak cases were too expensive to manufacture, and pistol containers became more utilitarian and cheaper. Many of the less expensive weapons made in the later part of the 19th century were sold in substantial cardboard boxes, and these often have makers' details and in-

Left

A German-made copy of the Colt Single Action Army Revolver, which looks real enough. It is, in fact, a blank firing copy, made so that it cannot be used to discharge a projectile, and it therefore requires no licence. Such pieces are popular with re-enactment groups.

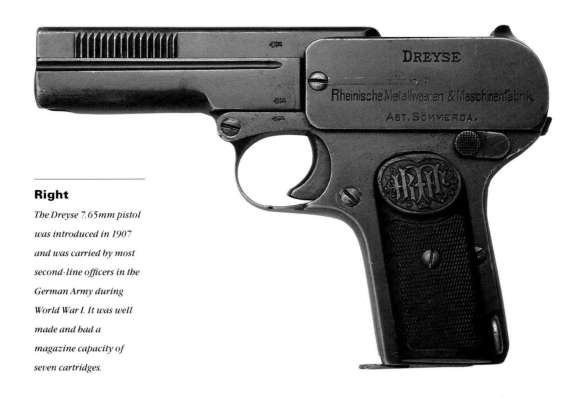

Right

The Dreyse 7.65mm pistol was introduced in 1907 and was carried by most second-line officers in the German Army during World War I. It was well made and had a magazine capacity of seven cartridges.

Right

Made in both 9mm and 7.65mm calibres, the Beretta Model 1915 has a manual safety catch mounted on the left-hand side. On the 9mm version the safety catch acted directly on the internal hammer. Production of this model apparently came to an end in 1919, but large numbers had been made by then, and this is not a rare item.

structions on use printed on the inside of the lid in place of the earlier trade labels. Other cardboard boxes held cartridges, and these, too, are worth looking out for.

Most modern gun manufacturers follow their predecessors and sell their products in substantial cardboard boxes, although some of the higher-priced weapons come in wooden boxes which are functional rather than decorative. Together with the box and the weapon, most manufacturers include a small pamphlet explaining how the gun functions and, sometimes, instructions on how to care for the new gun. These booklets will be the collectors' antiques of the future, and they should be collected and preserved. Some of these booklets from the earlier part of the 20th century included a fold-out sheet giving a labelled sectional view of the weapon.

Similar but larger and more detailed sheets were issued officially to the British Army armourers who were responsible for the care and repair of the weapons of their units. These sheets, together with the accompanying "Instructions for Armourers", are keenly collected. All armies issue instruc-

tion books of one kind or another, and many of them are concerned with the use and maintenance of handguns. Most of these were issued in large numbers, and they are reasonably available and cost little. During World War II, in preparation for an anticipated invasion by the Germans, a number of small instruction books were published in Britain to instruct non-military personnel in the rudiments of shooting, and most give a brief description of the weapons and how to use them. These, too, survive in quantity and are never expensive.

Shooting sports flourished at the end of the last century, and numerous official bodies, such as the National Rifle Association, were created by the shooters. As the sport was formalized a need arose for official rule books setting out the details of various courses of fire. Some sets of rules were issued annually, together with reviews of the past year's activities, and in most cases they were published in sufficient quantities to ensure that many have survived. Those that include details of the guns, targets, ammunition to be used, conditions of shooting positions and similar material are of especial interest.

Below

One of the smallest Beretta pistols ever made was the Model 950 .22in Short pistol, which was also available in 6.35mm calibre. Several minor variations were produced, and the original model number bore a variety of suffixes to denote these modifications. A number of these pistols were made in Brazil and, after 1978, in the United States, where it was also known as the Minx and the Jetfire.

Above

*For cleaning and
maintenance the barrel
catch of the Beretta Model
950 is moved so that the
barrel breaks down as
illustrated here.*

Targets are, by their very nature, disposable, but even so a few survive and are of interest, since they can reflect contemporary attitudes – some British targets from World War I feature Germans in spiked helmets, for example. Score books do not survive well, but there is a certain amount of interest in them when they do turn up.

Club photographs are always worth examining – not, perhaps, for the competitors, but for the weapons and conditions under which they shot. It is interesting to note that very few, if any, competitors appear to have worn any form of ear protectors in the early clubs, and this seems to have been the case even when shooting on indoor ranges. News photographs and contemporary magazines often contain photographs of some event or individual illustrating the handgun or associated equipment.

Prizes played a large part in competitive shooting, and cups and medals were the most usual. It was customary to present a cup, which was retained by the winner for a year, the winner's name being engraved on a plaque. Many were awarded by clubs which ceased to function when their membership faded away. The clubs' cups and medals were discarded, but they still turn up on the market and can form an interesting group of objects. Apart from the early 19th century medals, which seem to have been awarded only for musket and rifle shooting, there is not a great deal of interest in this type of medal. A few rare examples or those attributed to some well-known shooter may fetch high prices, but the majority of ordinary examples attract little interest.

Certificates of skill, high scores, attendance or other virtues were often awarded, and these too survive occasionally. The styles of printing and borders make some of them pleasant reminders of a past style.

Shooting club badges are also often found among the miscellaneous odds-and-ends boxes at fairs or markets and again seem to attract little interest. Some are woven cloth and others are pin-on enamel or metal badges.

7

Collecting and Care of Acquisitions

Below

The Savage Firearms Company of New York produced a number of self-loading pistols in several calibres. This Model 1917, which is 32in calibre, has a visible spur hammer. Over 14,000 were produced during the 1920s, and there is some interest in these weapons among collectors.

Legal Requirements There is one major problem for the would-be collector of handguns – the law. All countries feel that firearms are too dangerous to be uncontrolled and impose some limits on ownership. The one general exception made is in the matter of antiques, for law makers feel that the antique weapon does not pose a threat. Most countries allow a collector to keep as many antique firearms as desired, although a few insist that they be registered. The difficulty lies in defining the word antique – and for every definition, it is possible to find exceptions!

Attempts have been made to define antique firearms by the type of action, by the type of ammunition used and by the date of manufacture. Every system produces anomalies. In Britain it is possible to own a Colt Navy percussion revolver made in 1852 but not a copy made in Italy in 1982, but apart from the materials and some modifications for the purpose of manufacture, they are identical. It is assumed by the law makers that if somebody purchases a modern copy it is because they plan to fire it. In some countries of Europe the Snider rifle is regarded as an antique, but in others it is not. Some countries do not allow private individuals to own handguns that use military calibre ammunition, so that in some countries one may not own a pistol that fires 9mm Parabellum ammunition. However, if the cartridge case and breech are slightly modified the ammunition is no longer the same as the military cartridge and it is legal to own the gun. A British citizen may buy certain firearms abroad but may not take them home unless a special permit is obtained. The latest method being introduced in Britain is to declare that if a particular kind of ammunition is no longer available, the weapon with

Right

A British Army issue .38in revolver, which saw service in World War II. It looks a little worn and battered. Close inspection, however, will reveal that the firing pin is missing *from the hammer, and that the barrel is blocked and the cylinder has been made unusable. It is an officially deactivated weapon, freely available in Britain.*

which it was used may be considered an antique. While any relaxation in the law restricting ownership is welcome, the use of ammunition types as a guideline is going to make life very confusing and difficult for those who have to enforce the regulations.

There is one way of acquiring handguns that requires no licence, certificate or other legal requirement and that is to collect deactivated guns. In order to comply with the law, in Britain and some other countries, firearms can be rendered safe and incapable of firing. Externally they appear unchanged, but firing pins are removed, barrels blocked and sundry other changes made so they cannot, at least in theory, be reconverted. These deactivated weapons are not cheap, and most shooters and collectors do not approve of the changes made since the gun is ruined. However, there are those who argue that the process gives the enthusiast a chance to acquire items such as machine guns that would otherwise be totally unobtainable. In some countries the deactivation is much more fundamental and obvious. There is no doubt that there is a demand for such items,

certainly in Britain, for the number of deactivated weapons that has been sold is very high indeed.

In the USA laws vary from state to state, although there are some federal laws that apply to all the states.

With so many possible legal combinations and opinions the best advice to be given must be make sure that you inform yourself of the law for your area, state or country before even attempting to acquire your first handgun. The local police should be in a position to advise, but as firearm legislation is a complex subject it may be necessary to go to a fairly senior level to get reliable answers. Even then, the advice may be wrong. If possible, get a written statement setting out the position so that it is difficult for anyone to claim that they misunderstood your inten-

Above

These may look like a Luger 08 pistol and a P38, but they are, in fact, totally harmless copies. A large range of such "models" is available, many of which are made to fire blanks, and most are so realistic that they can be identified as replicas only when they are handled. Some are "soft air" weapons, which fire a harmless plastic pellet.

Right

These small vest pocket double barrelled-pistols are usually referred to as Derringers and were produced by many of the big manufacturers. They were available in single and double barrel versions and the usual calibre was .41in but other calibres were produced. These are from one of the smaller firearm manufacturers.

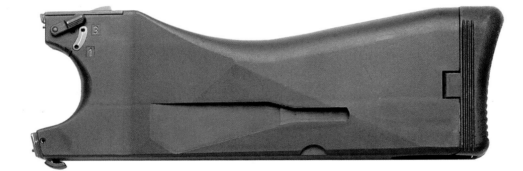

Left

One of the new style of self-loading pistols, the Heckler & Koch VP 70 9mm pistol has, like the Mauser and Luger, got a plastic stock, which can be attached to give greater stability when aiming. This German-made weapon has a large magazine capacity of 18 rounds, and it can be set to fire shots in bursts of three. For this reason its ownership is prohibited in some countries.

Below

The Heckler & Koch VP 70 is seen here with its holster/stock in position. The selector switch is set to the three-burst setting.

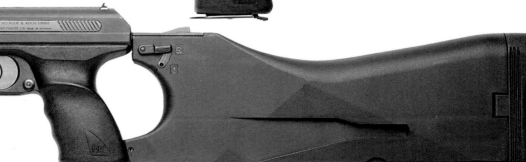

tions or did not say what you say they said! You should also contact any local or national societies involved with collecting or shooting because such societies are often better informed on the law than the police.

Care of Acquisitions Having cleared the first hurdle and found out that it is possible for you to collect the weapons, some preparation is necessary before you make your first acquisition. You must consider how you are going to store your collection, and some of the factors to be considered are security, recording and insurance.

Security Security is important because some police forces will insist on certain standards depending on the location and the likely size and nature of your proposed collection. The intrinsic value of the guns and the importance of preventing criminal use are both factors that make it essential that the guns are safely and securely protected.

Safes are an obvious storge point, but, of course, this means that the collection will not be seen on open display. Special cabinets with security glass doors and panels are available, and there are many types of alarm. Trigger locks can ensure that the actions are not worked, and, of course, ammunition and guns should never be kept together unless under strict supervision. Needless to say, all these precautions will cost money and sometimes the charges can be quite high.

Display Display and security are closely connected, and compromise is the usual solution. If the weapons are kept under glass it is important to ensure that they are not in direct sunlight, for the sun is a marvellous bleaching agent, lightening and drying the wood. Ideally, the weapons should not be handled with bare hands, for human sweat is a powerful rusting agent. Even present-day blueing is affected by some sweat, and thin cotton gloves should be worn at all times

Below

An engraving from the British publication The Graphic, *dating from 1881. It is interesting to see the traditional shooting position of the period. The bent arm was adequate for revolvers but would be inadequate for use with self-loading pistols. Items such as this are usually found by chance and are usually comparatively inexpensive.*

THE REIGN OF TERROR IN IRELAND—A LESSON IN THE ART OF SELF-DEFENCE.

Right

This rather cheap-looking weapon, the Liberator, was intended to play a part in the battles of World War II, to be dropped in quantities to various resistance groups fighting the Japanese in the Pacific. It is valued by some collectors as an oddity.

Above

The grips have been removed from this Colt Python .357in Magnum revolver to show the source of the power — the main spring, which forces the hammer down to strike the primer. The rib

along the top of the barrel helps to disperse the heat created by the shots, because the barrel can get very hot indeed.

Right

This curious looking weapon is a squeeze or palm pistol. It was designed to be held in the clenched fist, with the barrel projecting between the fingers. To fire a shot, the fist was clenched, which squeezed in the curved bar (the trigger) at the rear. The 8mm weapon, which was primarily intended as a

self-defence pistol, was named The Protector, and it was patented by a Frenchman, Turbiaux, in 1882. Unusual weapons such as this are popular with collectors.

when handling the weapons. The material on which the guns lie should be chemically inactive and certainly acid free.

Recording Having acquired an item for the collection the first job — after a quiet gloat — is to record the piece. It is well worth creating a fairly full catalogue right from the start of your collection. Quite apart from keeping a personal record, if the unfortunate should happen and an item be stolen, you will be able to provide your insurance company and the police with a full description. The important details to note are the small features that can distinguish one similar item from another. Numbers, marks, scratches, wear, measurements, weight and replacement parts can all help to identify a particular weapon.

The catalogue description will be greatly enhanced by the addition of a photograph, which ideally should be as detailed as possible — a tiny smudgy print will be of little help. One full-length shot together with one or two close-ups of any particular features will usually suffice. Modern Polaroid and SLR cameras are now so simple and effective that the taking of such photographs should not be too difficult.

Details of the price and place of purchase and subsequent disposal should all be recorded. In the interests of privacy it is as well to record the price by means of a simple code, substituting letters for figures.

Insurance In these uncertain times insurance is essential and there are companies who will insure collections. They will require a complete list of the items, with full descriptions and a valuation. It may be necessary to obtain an authenticated valuation from a professional, for which a charge will be made. In general, it is customary to fix the insurance about a third higher than actual value, for it is inevitable that the cost of replacing an item will exceed the original price paid.

Inevitably the question of insurance and values raises the question of what to pay for any item. The only realistic answer is as much as you want or can afford. There is never a set fixed price for a collector – even brand new pistols can be haggled over – and it is impossible to assign a specific price to every individual piece. There are so many variables. Scarcity and condition are two of the most important aspects to consider, but other factors are the amount of restoration, replacement or renovation that has been carried out and whether there are any special features about a particular weapon that make it especially desirable to the collector. All these and other points will need to be considered. If one of the books that lists values is used for reference, it must be remembered that the figures given will apply only to the particular item described or illustrated. In different circumstances a similar piece could sell at a very different price. All such lists are, and can only be, generalizations.

In the end, the question to be answered is how badly is the piece wanted. If there is a real desire, caution rather goes to the wall and a price in excess of the usual will be paid. To balance the feeling of consternation, it can be argued that if a particular piece was a little expensive at the time, in a year or so it will probably seem very reasonable.

Above

Carried by many French staff officers as their official side arm, Le Française 6.35mm pistol was not thought to be of much use in a military sense. The version illustrated here is Type Policeman, and it is rather unusual in that the movement of the slide does not cock the action. The movement of the trigger moves back the striker and releases it to fire the shot.

Below

Another slightly unusual feature of Le Fançaise was the forward-breaking movement of the barrel, although similar actions are found on other self-loaders.

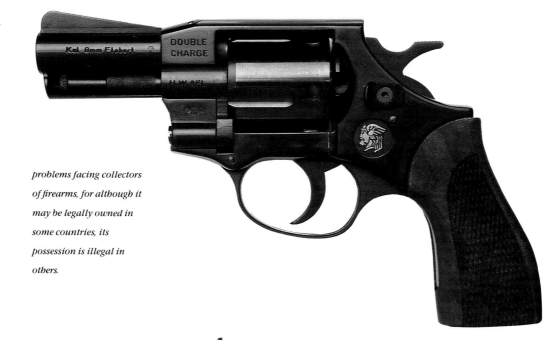

Right

This seemingly ordinary revolver is, in fact, rather unusual. It is a Flobert revolver, and the barrel has a central divide so that it cannot fire a solid shot. It was designed as a self-defence weapon, firing a cartridge containing a small charge of shot. This weapon is also an example of the problems facing collectors of firearms, for although it may be legally owned in some countries, its possession is illegal in others.

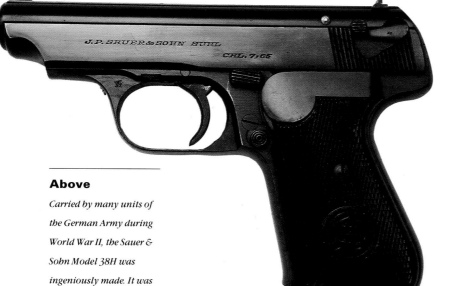

Above

Carried by many units of the German Army during World War II, the Sauer & Sohn Model 38H was ingeniously made. It was capable of being fired either single or double action. The internally mounted hammer could be raised or lowered by the external lever mounted on the left-hand side of the frame. Manufacture ceased at the end of the war, but the mechanism is of interest to collectors, and examples with Nazi markings are particularly keenly sought.

Checking Acquisitions After the piece has been thoroughly recorded it is time to inspect it in all its parts. Dismantling a modern hand-gun is, with one or two exceptions, fairly easy and straightforward, but there are a few basic rules that must be followed. The first, to which there can never be any excep-tion, is the proving of the weapon. This is the first thing to be done whenever a weapon is handled, and it simply means making sure that the weapon is unloaded. In the case of a revolver this means checking the cylinder to see that it is empty. With self-loading pistols

the magazine should be removed from the weapon and the slide pulled back to expose the breech to ensure that there is not a round in place. While this is being done the weapon should always be pointed in a safe direction so that should there be an accidental discharge there is no chance of anybody being hit.

Although most revolvers are similar in construction, there are so many types and the self-loading pistols have such a great variety of catches and locking springs that it is essential to check before beginning the dismantling process. Several books give sectionalized and diagrammatic views as well as advice on the correct procedures. These should be consulted and the instruc-tions followed carefully. It is good policy to put the parts on a lid or tray to minimize the chances of their falling onto the floor, and if they are placed in sequence as they are removed this will facilitate replacement.

The tools required are fairly minimal, but the golden rule is that screwdrivers, turn-screws, of the appropriate size must always be used – too large or too small a blade can slip to produce a nasty scratch, and although it is possible to touch up scratches with

Above

This sturdy military pistol was carried by Austrian forces. It is the 1912 Steyr Hahn model, and the example illustrated was made in 1916. The magazine was fixed and loaded from a clip of cartridges inserted from *the top. It was a particularly strong pistol, which used a powerful cartridge. Apart from the army of the Austro-Hungarian Empire, it was also used by the armed forces of Romania and Chile, and a few were re-* *barrelled to take the 9mm Parabellum cartridge. Approximately 250,000 were made and many have survived, but only those with unusual markings are likely to be highly sought after.*

various patent commercial compounds, it is better to avoid them rather than cure them. Cleaning and oiling will probably be all that is required, and the use of silicone cloths to wipe over the weapon after re-assembly is not a bad idea.

Acquiring Handguns When security has been planned and any permission required has been obtained, it is time to acquire your first piece.

A feature of the post-war collecting scene has been the growing number of arms fairs held in many countries. These are invaluable for collectors for, quite apart from the opportunity to buy, they offer the chance to look. The more specimens one sees and handles, the greater the experience gained and the better qualified the collector becomes and the more able to judge an item.

There are three main sources of supply – dealers, auction houses and fellow collectors.
Dealers Always remember that a dealer is in the business to make a profit and will seek to sell for more than he or she paid. You are paying for the dealer's trouble and expertise.

Good dealers will give good service and take only a reasonable profit. They will also guarantee that the object sold is exactly as described, and if no such guarantee is forthcoming, look for dealers who will supply one. Dealers have time to attend shows, visit auctions and follow up interesting leads, which all take up time the average collector does not usually have, and dealers can, therefore, have an important place in the collector's life.

Above

This version of the Mauser Broomhandle was known as the Bolo Mauser, since it was popular in Bolshevik Russia. It has a shorter barrel and a generally smaller frame than normal. This particular example is a very late model. Some Broomhandle pistols are found with a red figure 9 branded on the butt to indicate that they fire 9mm ammunition.

Right

This 7.65mm pistol from the Spanish firearms manufacturing centre at Eibar was made by Garate Anitua. Spain has a reputation for producing good quality weapons, and in considerable numbers. In 1908, for example, more than 250,000 firearms were produced in Eibar.

Below

A civilian version of the .32in Webley pistol. This example is in very fine condition and retains much of its original colour, a feature that is also attractive to collectors. The list of numbers of the pistols produced has survived, and it can be deduced that this model was made in March 1912, which makes it a fairly early example. There were minor differences between the Police and the civilian versions.

Below

The Stevens Arms Company of Chicopee Falls, Massachusetts, was renowned for its single shot pistols, many of which were described as "pocket rifles" because they were designed to be used with a detachable skeleton stock. Early examples of the company's weapons are sought after, production continued until 1942, and later models are less desirable.

Right

Most firearms produced by the Stevens Arms Company were top-break models, with the barrel folding down as here. Many of the company's early firearms are .22in calibre.

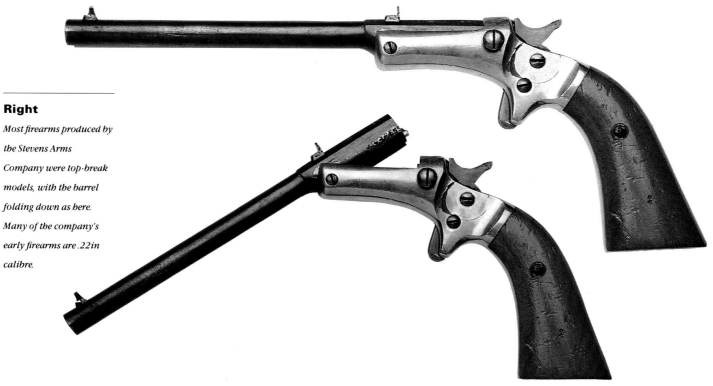

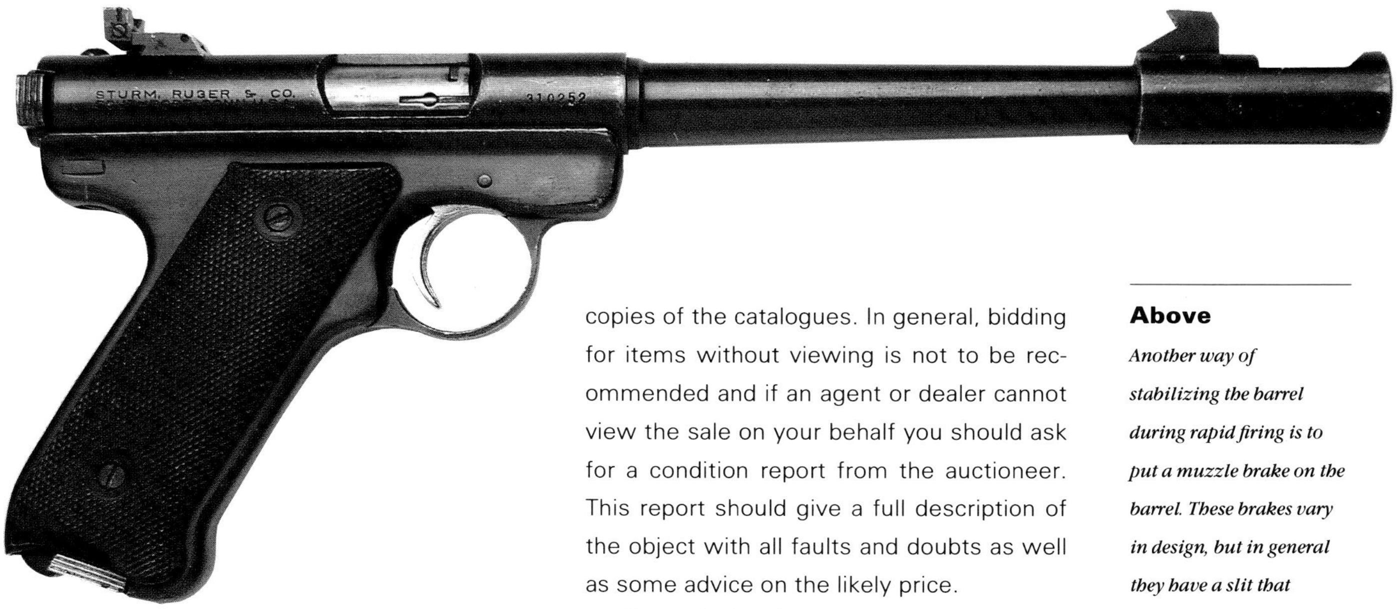

Auction Houses You should bear in mind that most of a dealer's stock will be purchased at auction, and if you, too, buy at auction, you will save money by cutting out the dealer's profit. Auction houses depend on their reputation and expertise to attract business, so the fact that an object is offered for auction suggests that it is probably correct. However, no one is infallible and mistakes do occur, but auction houses usually have clauses in their terms and conditions that will allow the purchaser to claim back the cost if an object is found to be not as catalogued. It is always wise to keep an eye on the list of forthcoming sales and to obtain copies of the catalogues. In general, bidding for items without viewing is not to be recommended and if an agent or dealer cannot view the sale on your behalf you should ask for a condition report from the auctioneer. This report should give a full description of the object with all faults and doubts as well as some advice on the likely price.

If you decide that an item in an auction is of interest, it is important to determine the top bid you are prepared to make. Many auction houses offer estimates, which is their guess at what the object will sell for, and more often than not they will be right. Bearing this in mind and considering the cash you have available, you must decide on the maximum price that you are prepared to bid and keep to that figure. Auctions seem to have a peculiar effect on people, possibly produced by proximity to other bidders – runaway bidding. If the projected top figure is passed, it can be disastrous to think that one more bid will get the lot. Your one more bid is as likely as not leading to someone

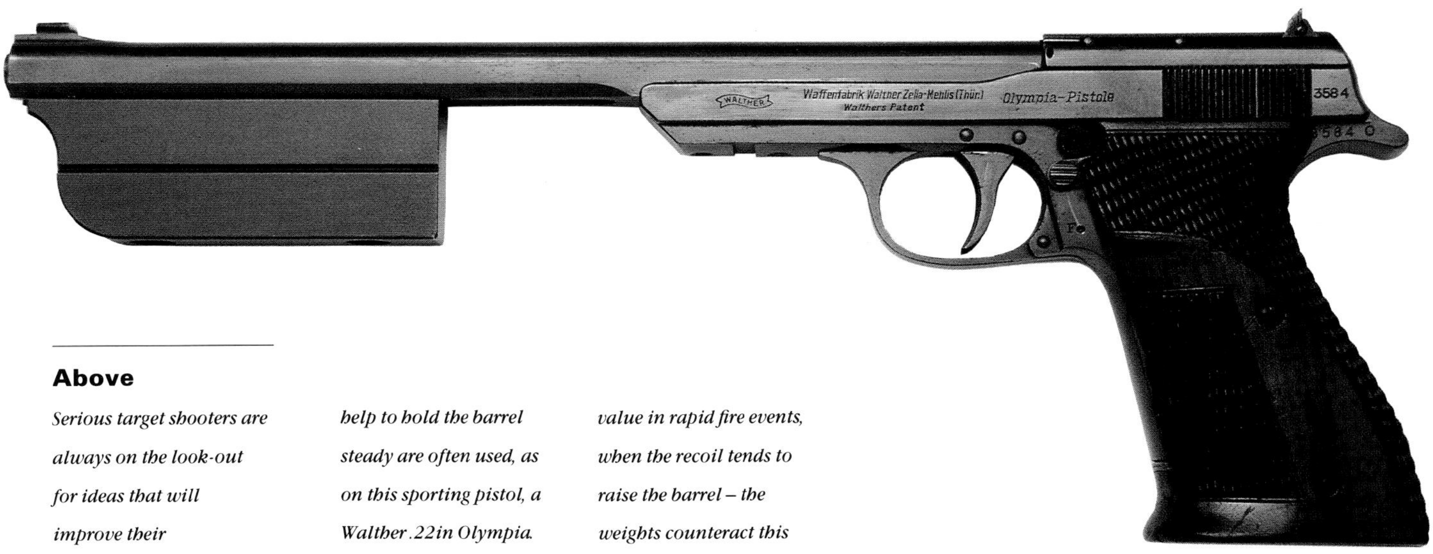

Above

Another way of stabilizing the barrel during rapid firing is to put a muzzle brake on the barrel. These brakes vary in design, but in general they have a slit that allows some of the gas to escape in a direction that counteracts the recoil. The Mark 1 Ruger .22in LR pistol shown here has just such a device fitted, and it is still available.

Above

Serious target shooters are always on the look-out for ideas that will improve their performance. Weights that help to hold the barrel steady are often used, as on this sporting pistol, a Walther .22in Olympia. The weights are of most value in rapid fire events, when the recoil tends to raise the barrel – the weights counteract this effect.

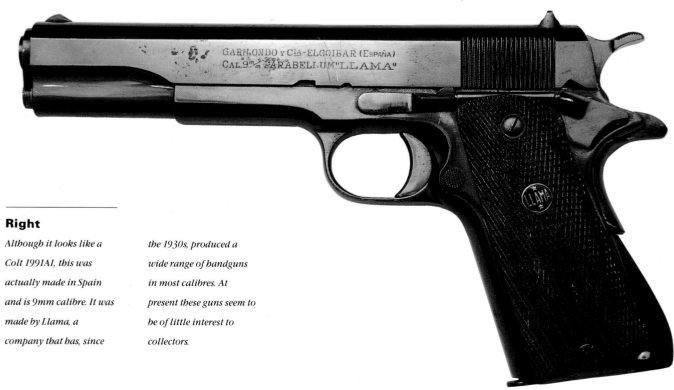

Right

Much target shooting is done with small calibre weapons such as this Hi-Standard Model B .22in pistol. It has a long barrel, which helps accurate shooting because the sights are set some distance apart, and this, in turn, makes for a better sight picture. The pistol was produced for about 10 years from 1932, and it is not, therefore, too common. Good examples will be in demand.

else's one more bid, and the price begins to rise – this leads to another bid from you, and suddenly you are paying much more than you intended. Regular bidders can sometimes assess when one more bid will do, but it takes time and experience to judge the situation correctly.

Collectors Experience is vital to the collector and one way of speeding up its acquisition is to meet other collectors. There are many societies and clubs devoted to the collecting, study and use of handguns, and contact with these groups is always worthwhile. The exchange of information, the chance to see collections and the buying and selling that takes place among the members make the cost of the subscription a good investment. Many antique fairs offer space to such societies, which is another reason for attending such events. Trips to various museums and exhibitions are never wasted, either, since every visit can add something to the knowledge and understanding of the subject.

Right

Although it looks like a Colt 1991A1, this was actually made in Spain and is 9mm calibre. It was made by Llama, a company that has, since the 1930s, produced a wide range of handguns in most calibres. At present these guns seem to be of little interest to collectors.

Care of the collection is obviously important for damage and wear will reduce the value in varying degrees. Restoration and repairs usually have the same effect as most collectors prefer the items to be in as original condition as possible. Snapping the action of revolvers is dangerous because it can damage the hammer, nipples and springs, and actions should not be left cocked, for the continual tension on the springs may cause fractures. It is also not good policy to leave pistols in holsters, especially leather ones, for reactions between the leather and metal can damage the surface of the metal. Treated with care and respect, a collection will give hours of pleasure and may also represent a surprisingly valuable investment in times to come.

Left

Firms, such as Lyman, produce compact tool kits which are very suitable for simple repairs and maintenance. The ratchet screwdriver, seen here, is designed to take a variety of blades – a vital factor when working with firearms, as it is essential to use only the correct size each time.

Further Reading

Reference books are essential for the collector. The number of books devoted to handguns and associated topics that has been published in recent years is vast, and today's collectors have a wealth of information at their fingertips that earlier collectors could only dream about.

Ideally, collectors should have books of two main types. The first group, antiquarian books, consists of those early works on the subject that, although possibly out of date in some respects, still contain a great deal of valuable information that is not obtainable elsewhere. The second type of books, working reference volumes, is more problematical, for such a huge number of books has been published on the subject in recent years that only collectors with virtually unlimited resources can hope to add them all to their libraries.

Listed below are some of the best written, most informative and reliable titles. The list is by no means exhaustive, and the fact that a title is not included is no more than a recognition that both space and resources are limited.

Antiquarian Books

The date and place of first publication is shown here. However, many books have been reprinted, and it is always worth keeping an eye on specialist publishers' stock lists.

Blanch, H. J., *A Century of Guns*, London, 1909
Dove, P. E., *The Revolver*, Edinburgh, 1858
Greener, W., *The Gun*, London, 1835
Greener, W. W., *Modern Breech-Loaders*, London, 1871
   The Gun and its Development (9th edition), London, 1916

Pollard, H. B. C., *The Book of the Pistol and Revolver*, London, 1917
Thierbach, M., *Die Geschichtliche Entwicklung Der Handfeuerwaffen*, Dresden, 1886
Winans, W., *The Art of Revolver Shooting*, London and New York, 1901

Reference Books

Albaugh, W., Bonet, H. and Simmons, E., *Confederate Handguns*, Pennsylvania, 1963
Brady, D. B., *Colt Automatic Pistols*, California, 1973
Barnes, F., *Cartridges of the World*, 1980
Bianchi, J., *Blue Steel and Gun Leather*, Dallas, 1978
Boothroyd, G., *The Hand Gun*, London, 1978
Bruce, G., *Webley and Scott Automatic Pistols*, Zurich, 1992
Bruce, G. and Reinhart, C., *Webley Revolvers*, Zurich, 1988
Byron, D., *Gunmarks*, New York, 1979
Caydiou, Y. and Richard, A., *Modern Firearms*, London, 1977
Chamberlain, W. and Taylerson, A., *Adams' Revolvers*, London, 1976; *Revolvers of the British Services 1854–1954*, Bloomfield, 1989
Costanza, S., *World of Lugers* (volume 1), Ohio, 1977
Cope, K., *Stevens Pistols and Pocket Rifles*, Ontario, 1971
Derby, H., *The Hand Cannons of Imperial Japan*, North Carolina, 1981
Daw, G. H., *Gun Patents* (reprint), Bath, 1973
Edwards, W. B., *Story of Colts' Revolver*, Harrisburg, 1957
Ezell, E., *Handguns of the World*, London 1981
Flayderman, N., *Guide to Antique American Firearms* (4th edition), Northbrook, 1988
Gluckman, A., *United States Martial Pistols and Revolvers*, Harrisburg, 1960
Goddard, W. H., *The Government Models*, Rhode Island, 1988
Graham, R., Kopec, J. and Moore, C., *A Study of the Colt Single Action Army Revolver*, Dallas, 1976
Hogg, I. V., *German Pistols and Revolvers 1871–1945*, London 1971
Hogg, I. V. and Wilson, R., *Textbook of Automatic Pistols*, London, 1975
Jinks, R., *History of Smith & Wesson*, North Hollywood, 1977
Josserand, M. and Stevenson, I., *Pistols, Revolvers and Ammunition*, New York, 1972
Karr, C. and Karr, R., *Remington Handguns*, New York, 1960
Koch, R., *The FP .45 Liberator Pistol 1942–45*, US, 1976
Logan, H., *Cartridges*, New York, 1953
Mathews, J. H., *Firearms Identification* (3 volumes), Springfield, Massachusetts, 1973
Moore, C. K., *Single Action Army Revolvers and the London Agency*, Rhode Island, 1990
Murtz, A. (ed), *Exploded Firearm Drawings* (3rd edition), Northfield, 1981
Peterson, H., *The Remington Historical Treasury of American Guns*, New York, 1966
Phillips, P. and Wilson, R. L., *Paterson Colt Pistol Variations*, Dallas, 1979
Roberts, D. and Bristow, A., *An Introduction to Modern Police Firearms*, California, 1969
Sellers, F. and Smith, S. E., *American Percussion Revolvers*, Ontario, 1971
Smith, G., and Curtis, C., *The Pinfire System*, San Francisco, 1983
Smith, W. H., *Pistols and Revolvers*, Harrisburg, 1968
Smith, W. H. *Mauser, Walther and Mannlicher Firearms*, Harrisburg, 1971
Sutherland, R. Q. and Wilson, R., *The Book of Colt Firearms*, Kansas City, 1971
Suydam, C., *The American Cartridge*, California, 1960
Taylerson, A., *The Revolver 1865–1888*, London 1966
Taylerson, A., *The Revolver 1889–1914*, London 1970
Taylerson, A., Andrews, R. and Frith, J., *The Revolver 1818–1865*, London, 1968
Walter, J., *Luger*, London 1977
Weston, P. B., *Handbook of Handgunning*, New York, 1968
White, H. and Munshall, B., *Cartridge Headstamp Guide*, Maryland, 1977
Wilkinson, F., *World's Great Guns*, London, 1977
Wood, J. B., *Beretta Automatic Pistols*, Harrisburg, 1985

Index